"Mental (telepathy) is not a jest but a fact, and it is a thing not rare, but exceedingly common."

Mark Twain

Mark Twain described the contents of an unopened letter. George Bernard Shaw suffered from a telepathic "curse." Bell Telephone secretly hired the talents of a New Jersey psychic.

Whether about famous or ordinary people, the authentic cases presented in this book show that messages can be transmitted from one person to another *by the mind alone*. Each true episode is living proof of the mind's strange powers, a mystery that may someday be penetrated by science as it searches the unknown depth of man's nature.

TRUE EXPERIENCES IN TELEPATHY

Edited by

MARTIN EBON

A SIGNET MYSTIC BOOK
Published by The New American Library

First Printing, November, 1967

SIGNET TRADEMARK REG. U.S. PAT. OFF. AND FOREIGN COUNTRIES
REGISTERED TRADEMARK—MARCA REGISTRADA
HECHO EN CHICAGO, U.S.A.

SIGNET MYSTIC BOOKS are published by
The New American Library, Inc.,
1301 Avenue of the Americas, New York, New York 10019

PRINTED IN THE UNITED STATES OF AMERICA

CONTENTS

INTRODUCTION

The Case for Telepathy

Some people have called it thought transference, others think of it as mind reading, but most of us refer to it as telepathy. What exactly is it? No one really knows. However, there is now very little doubt that it does occur, and virtually all the time. Yet, like so much else about the human personality and the human mind, scientific investigation still has not shown how telepathy works, what stimulates or retards it. The science of parapsychology, which investigates telepathy and other unusual phenomena, is relatively young. There is much, therefore, in telepathic events that we do not quite understand.

But we do know, from a great number of case histories, as well as from scientific experimentation, that telepathy functions in many ways: from mind to mind, from mind to event or object. The stories in this volume concern different settings and personalities. They are broadly representative of the experiences that many people encounter in their daily life, although they often do not notice them, or they forget them, or they just don't care to talk about them. In our supposedly ordered society, a telepathic experience, when it is brought out in conversation, only too often is met by embarrassed smiles. Still, most people either have had telepathic experiences or know someone who has them, perhaps frequently.

The scientific vocabulary that has developed around these phenomena allows for making certain distinctions. *Telepathy,* strictly speaking, is the perceiving of an impression at the same time that someone else perceives it. *Clairvoyance,* a variant of this experience, is the apparent "seeing" of a distant event or object itself, rather than the observing of it through the senses, or mind of another person. It is not always possible to tell the two apart. When a mother has a sudden flash of fear that her child is drowning, then runs out of the cottage and finds that her daughter is actually struggling with the undertow—has she, as it were, tuned in on her child's panic? Did the girl's fear become a call of anguish that the mother heard extrasensorially? Or did she, in her mind's eye, perceive the actual waves breaking over the child? It may have been one or the other, or a mixture of both. Parapsychologists cover a variety of such elements in the catch-all category of GESP (General Extra-Sensory Perception).

The one category of telepathy that is most common—and the case just cited represents it—is *crisis telepathy*. Disasters, accidents, or death are frequent subjects of crisis telepathy. Another common category is telepathy in *dreams*. As you will see in the following accounts, many instances of telepathy occur in the waking stage. Still, telepathic dreams are among the most frequent psychic phenomena reported, in individual cases and in the literature of parapsychology. The editor of this volume discussed the frequency of such cases in a paper, "Parapsychological Dream Studies," at the international conference on "The Dream and Human Societies," which took place in France in June, 1962, stating that "Parapsychological dream studies call for unusual qualities of research: detached, scientific, cerebral preparation and execution of investigation or experiment; sensitive understanding of the delicate, the deeply emotion-laden, traditionally magical that may lie at the root of not yet understood phenomena. To strike a balance between detachment and understanding, between the scholar's role as an outsider and as participant—that is the challenge that gives this work its unique demanding quality."

Scientific investigation of telepathy must always be aware that laboratory techniques designed to control experimentation in this field may endanger the spontaneity of the experience. That is why case histories, such as those that follow, provide the basic material on which key studies have to be based. When we speak of case histories, we mean the kind of human experience in telepathy that has been recorded since biblical times and can be found in records unearthed by archaeologists that go back even further, to the Babylonian and Etruscan periods. In religious traditions of all faiths, thought transference plays a role; indeed, some modern theologians familiar with parapsychological research regard prayer as a form of telepathy, between man and God.

Not only scholarly literature, but fiction as well, has taken cognizance of telepathy. Lovers separated by geography have often been pictured as communicating with each other by thought. Almost everyone can cite instances when he was about to pick up the telephone to call another person, just as the phone rang; the expression, "Oh, I was just about to call you!" is almost as common as a greeting in everyday life. In recent years, research has pointed to particularly strong telepathic links between mother and child, notably during the first few months of a baby's life; this has been documented by electroencephalographic patterns of the dreams of mothers and their children, where similarities point to an extrasensory relationship.

No one knows whether emotional empathy or hostility are at the bottom of certain telepathic experiences. Perhaps both are, because they can express ambivalent but strong interpersonal relations. Experiments with close relatives or persons otherwise emotionally and environmentally attached to each other have yielded positive results in this field. Scientific controversy grows especially lively when it comes to the experiences of, and experiments with, twins, notably identical twins. Case histories showing a telepathic link between such twins are striking, but laboratory experiments have failed to bear out these claims. Nevertheless, it is obviously too early to define all the factors that permit telepathy to operate.

There is general agreement, however, that emotional elements are involved whenever thought transference seems to occur. The collection of extrasensory phenomena of all types, including telepathic experiences, was given new impetus at the international Conference on Spontaneous Phenomena, in Cambridge, England, in 1956. The meeting, sponsored by the Society of Psychical Research (London) and the Parapsychology Foundation (New York) was under the chairmanship of Dr. Gardner Murphy, Director of Research at the Menninger Clinic (Topeka, Kansas). The participants worked out international standards for the collection, investigation, and documentation of telepathic cases and other phenomena. Efforts were also made to introduce psychological techniques into study methods. Pioneer work in this particular area has been done by Dr. Emilio Servadio (Rome). President of the Italian Society of Psycho-Analysis. The following summary of a case he recorded involving a telepathic dream illustrates Dr. Servadio's psychological form of approach.

Dr. Servadio reported that, on the night of April 23, a sixteen-year-old girl whom he called Luisa dreamt that the mother of her fiancé, Guido, was wearing an unusual, silver ring on her finger. Engravings on the ring's surface resembled hieroglyphics. The ring could be opened, and Luisa thought that it contained perfume. When she woke up, she told her mother about the dream. Meanwhile, her fiancé had returned from a trip to the International Fair at Milan. When Luisa telephoned and started to tell him about her dream, a few hours later, Guido interrupted her and told her excitedly that he had brought just such a ring with him to Rome. He had bought it at the Somali Pavilion of the Fair and had given it to his mother. When she heard this, Luisa dropped the phone and put her mother on to confirm the dream as she had related it to her. Dr. Servadio vouches for all these details, which he noted down shortly after they occurred. He describes the psychological setting within which this telepathic dream occurred—and which apparently made it possible—as follows:

> Luisa and Guido were engaged to be married and very much in love. Their engagement was still unofficial, but Luisa was eager to become formally and publicly engaged to Guido. She looked forward to the day when he would present her with an engagement ring. Luisa's father had died when she was still an infant. She was brought up by her mother and also cared for by her mother's three sisters. No male figure played any prominent role in her childhood. Her mother was remarried in 1951, when Luisa was eleven years old.

According to Dr. Servadio, the Oedipus complex—a daughter's attraction to her father and resentment of her mother—was "quite notable" in Luisa's life situation, and she showed strong enthusiasms about prominent men and an unfriendly attitude toward her mother and "maternal figures" generally. He adds:

> Luisa was aware of Guido's attachment to, and respect for, his mother. She also knew that he would visit the Milan Fair. Possibly, she expected Guido to bring her a present, which he actually did—although it was not a ring for her finger, but a pair of earrings. Probably because of oedipal attachment of his own, he selected a ring for his mother and not for Luisa. One might say that, being emotionally attached to two women at the same time, Guido showed a preference for his mother, by bringing her a ring, while selecting for Luisa a nice but much less significant present. He probably had no intention of concealing from Luisa the fact that he had bought a ring for his mother.

The ring, as Dr. Servadio sees it, had become a focus of the "ambiguous ethical situation" between the two young people and Guido's mother, symbolizing the "psychological obstacles" which delayed the official engagement. Dr. Servadio concludes:

> Luisa broke through this obstacle by means of telepathy. She was able to establish a temporary symbolism between Guido and herself and to merge in an unconscious psychic world, which comprised them both. She was thus able to express, in her dream, her insurmountable rivalry toward the mother figure, including her hostility based on the fact that her own mother, and not she, had been subject to an experience involving engagement and marriage. Through her dream, she could tell her own mother of Guido's preference for his mother, and of the wrong he had thus done his sweetheart.

It is interesting to note that the Italian psychoanalyst said that Luisa "broke through" an obstacle when she had the telepathic dream. Such a breaking-through seems to occur in virtually every example of thought transference. Sigmund Freud, founder of psychoanalysis, thought that telepathy might be an archaic factor, something that man has retained imperfectly from his animal ancestors; other scholars hold similar views, but telepathy may also involve extrasensory qualities that are gaining in strength in man's evolution, or that can be learned and perfected.

Based on observations of case histories, laboratory experiments in telepathy have provided statistical documentation. This work was begun by Dr. J. B. Rhine and his associates at the Parapsychology Laboratory of Duke University in the 1930's. Their study, now in its fourth decade, has produced a large body of research data on every aspect of quantitative study in telepathy. Dr. Rhine, speaking at London's Guildhall in October, 1965, illustrated the link between case histories in telepathy and laboratory experiment. Speaking at the invitation of the British Association for the Advancement of Science, he cited the dream of an American scholar working in China, a "Dr. C." This woman was awakened one night when she heard her name called by the voice of her mother, who was then in Vermont. Dr. C. was sufficiently awake to note the time of this deeply disturbing experience. In due course, Dr. Rhine said, "she learned that her mother, who was dying at the time of this happening, had been asking for her."

When it came to translating this type of experience into a laboratory experiment, Dr. Rhine found that the clairvoyance type—in which the subject somehow "sees" one of the ESP cards himself, rather than through the eyes of another person—was easier to handle than the telepathic type. (ESP cards have five symbols: cross, square, circle, wavy lines, and triangle.) Nevertheless, telepathy has played a major part in these experiments, as one category of extrasensory perception overlaps another. An extensive literature in this field exists, and any reader interested in it can obtain background pamphlets and bibliographical information by writing either to Dr. Rhine's Foundation for Research on the Nature of Man,

College Station, Durham, North Carolina 27708, or to the Parapsychology Foundation, 29 West 57th Street, New York, N.Y. 10019.

Current information on telepathy experiments is contained in the *Journal of Parapsychology,* Durham; the *International Journal of Parapsychology,* New York; and in the *Journals* of the American and British Societies for Psychical Research, in New York and London respectively. Libraries list books in this field under "Parapsychology" or "Psychical Research," as well as under "Telepathy."

The periodicals in this field have, in recent years, carried a number of reports of apparently strikingly successful telepathy experiments carried out by Dr. Milan Ryzl, a research worker in Prague, Czechoslovakia. His laboratory work is of particular interest, as he combines hypnosis with telepathy: his subject, Pavel Stepanek, built up an excellent record in telepathic experiments while in a hypnotic trance. This is not the only example of increasing attention paid to telepathy research in eastern European countries. Throughout the 1960's, Russian researchers have shown consistent interest in telepathy experiments. The dean of modern Russian parapsychology, Dr. Leonid L. Vasiliev, died in 1966 at the age of seventy-four. He had set up a laboratory at the University of Leningrad, where physiological aspects of parapsychology are still being examined today. A new center of research in this area was established in Moscow in 1966 in the A. S. Popov Scientific-Technological Society of Radiotechnology and Electrocommunication.

One interesting theoretical aspect of Soviet studies in parapsychology is the effort to relate it to the question of religion. Briefly put, the researchers seek to use material proof of psychic phenomena as an antireligious argument: if such events can be proved to happen, they maintain, they are part of everyday science, and not religious or miraculous. The type of telepathic experience recorded in Russia shows how universal these events are. A case recorded in the Moscow magazine *Science and Religion,* reported by a member of a Soviet submarine crew, describes an impression of fear and drowning, at the very moment that one of his crew mates had drowned;

the drowned seaman had been working on top of the submarine as it submerged and it had sucked him under.

The arguments for and against telepathy, as the ones for and against other aspects of parapsychological research, are about the same in the Soviet Union and other east European countries as they are in the West. Put simply, skeptics maintain that people are merely dramatizing events that are pure coincidence, or that laboratory techniques are imperfect. Letters-to-the-editor of Soviet magazines dealing with this subject read very much like those published in periodicals in the United States or Europe. Those who argue in favor of research in telepathy and related phenomena often say simply that criticism is welcome; that all scientific investigation has to go through a period of questioning and self-questioning; and that it is better to record, experiment, and analyze, than it is to scorn what you know nothing about, what apparently simply doesn't interest you—or that of which you are afraid.

To the average person, the most telling argument is a personal experience or that of a close friend or relative. Even researchers working with statistical material are often most deeply impressed by a telepathic experience of their own—one so striking and personal that it simply can't be argued away.

Telepathic experiences, such as those included in this volume, have been observed here in the United States as well as abroad, by prominent persons and people in every walk of life, by men and women, in the present and the past. There is a striking sameness about these experiences. Surveys made in the United States, Great Britain, Holland, Scandinavia, Germany, Switzerland, and elsewhere have shown a close correlation between the categories of experiences recorded. Just about anyone, anywhere is likely to have a telepathic experience. Those who say that they have more than the average may be more alert, more telepathically "gifted," or simply more inclined to talk about their experiences than others.

Pioneer work has also been done in telepathy among animals. The Rhine laboratory has, for several years, kept records on cases called "psi trailing" (the Greek letter "psi" is used to identify a parapsychological experience). There are numerous cases documenting, say, a dog trailing his owner from a far distance, in the manner of a carrier pigeon returning to its roost. Typical, too, is a dog's apparent awareness of his owner's fate—it howls or whimpers when some misfortune befalls its master; this is "crisis telepathy" in another form.

What are the frontiers of telepathy today?

The relationship between telepathy and hypnosis has been pushed into the foreground by Dr. Ryzl's successful experiments in Czechoslovakia. Actually, other hypnosis research has lagged, been limited either to stage magic or become a substitute for anesthesia in dentistry or childbirth. Now, telepathy has placed hypnosis in a new and prominent light. Russian experimenters have sought to use telepathy in developing hypnosis-at-a-distance. In these experiments, the subject is given the telepathic command to go into a hypnotic trance while the hypnotist is in another part of a building, or even farther away.

Telepathy, as you can see, is thus moving in many directions. Modern scientific methods are being brought to bear on an ancient experience. In New York, for instance, Dr. Gertrude Schmeidler, of the Department of Psychology at City College, is utilizing a computer to record and calculate telepathic results. A psychiatrist, Dr. Montague Ullman of Maimonides Hospital in Brooklyn, is engaged in a series of experiments designed to induce telepathy in dreams. This is being done by exposing a target picture, such as a painting, to a participant or agent in the experiment, while the subject is asleep in another room. The dreams of the subject are recorded to see whether they correspond with the target picture on which the agent has been concentrating. This research is carefully controlled, extends over several years, and provides well-documented results.

With all these experiments going on, one might ask, Just what good is it to examine telepathy? Or, as Dr. Rhine asked in his London lecture, "ESP—What Can We Make of It?" He replied that science must take "from the shelf of the supernatural" events that can be subjected to scholarly examination, in order to gain greater insight into the nature of man himself. And while the Russians may want to prove the physical realtity of telepathy in order to disprove religious concepts, is it not possible that proof of the so-called miraculous may actually provide scientific arguments in support of the very phenomena on which major religions are based? Rhine recalls that "all the natural phenomena known to ancient man were wrapped in the same fog of religious mystery that encompassed his life." Gradually, the sciences have emerged to penetrate the mysteries of lightning, volcano, earthquake, sunrise, birth and death. As Rhine says, they have "developed such control over life and health as completely to overshadow the powers the ancients conceded to their all-powerful deities; and now we turn the exploring skills of scholarship upon the remaining zone of the mysteries of man's own hidden nature. . . ."

But must we? Must we really know more? Have we not discovered enough? These are questions everyone must answer for himself, the scientist most of all. Is there a danger, perhaps, that a force such as telepathy may be manipulated, focused, directed for ill as well as good? Could it be an instrument of warfare? Might it be used to communicate with submarines or astronauts? These questions have been asked, and partial answers can be recorded. Although governments may enter the research field of telepathy—as a form of communication, "mind reading," or intelligence—the nature of these phenomena makes them too elusive for such exploitation. That is probably just as well. In this age of brainwashing and of invasion of privacy through electronic eavesdropping devices, the last thing we'd want would be mind invasion by telepathy. Being spontaneous, elusive, and difficult to control renders telepathy a particularly challenging subject of research—but it also keeps us safe from telepathic intrusion.

Telepathy is of inherent interest to all of us—whether we admit it or not. It stands in the fascinating no-man's-land of human knowledge, offering the promise of new and significant insight into ourselves.

MARTIN EBON

New York, August 1967

A baffled police force in Edmonton, Alberta, Canada with four murders and no clues, sat up in amazement when the little doctor began reading the suspect's thoughts

A MURDER CASE

Police Chief Michael Gier (Retired)
As told to
Kurt Singer

I was wallowing in the depths of frustration and despair. As police chief, I stood at the top of our organization, making a perfect target for hot criticism. And at that phase of the Booher case, I was hearing such scathing adjectives as "inefficient," "sluggish," and "incompetent" from the public, and "zany," "crazy," and "nuts" from my own colleagues.

I admit, in retrospect, that my methods were unorthodox, to say the least. I can understand the white and silent rage with which Detective Jim Leslie accepted my assignment to meet the train at the Edmonton railway station and bring Dr. Maximilian Langsner of Vienna back to my office.

Leslie was a successful detective with numerous kudos to his account, much praise for his careful and painstaking methods, and a clear record of past successes. The fact remained, however, that he had not found one clue, one motive or one bit of evidence that would help unravel the mass murder at the Booher farm.

Dr. Langsner was either a marvel or a hoax. I will leave it to the reader to judge. I will simply tell the tale as it happened.

The Viennese doctor had first come to my attention as a result of his unaccountable activities in Vancouver, British Columbia. He had walked into police headquarters there and announced without so much as a hesitating blink of his sharp black eyes that he could solve a jewel robbery that was baffling the authorities. He said he would lead the police to the jewels.

The Vancouver police, as skeptical as Detective Leslie was now, nevertheless granted Langsner's request to be placed in the cell with the robbery suspect.

Dr. Langsner stood stiffly in one corner of the small room. Never did he ask a question or make an overture to the suspected thief. After thirty minutes of silence, the doctor left the cell and announced to the incredulous group of police officers, "The stolen jewels are hidden behind a picture in a room with yellow walls."

The Vancouver police muttered among themselves, for they had searched and re-searched the room of the suspect's girl friend—which had, incidentally, yellow walls.

"Musta read it in the papers," was their opinion. But they took a third look, and found the missing jewels secreted under the wallpaper behind the picture.

This was the first of three cases that the strange little mop-headed man had solved in Canada.

The cases seem to have been solved by a kind of telepathy, an inner receptivity that seemed to give Dr. Langsner the weird and unbelievable ability to read another's thoughts. When I finally asked him how he did it, he shrugged and said, "I do not know. Some have the power, others do not. I call it brain waves."

Detective Leslie was less impressed than he was angry when he saw the quaint stooped figure of the Viennese doctor totter from the train, carrying an umbrella and a small piece of scarred luggage, and looking around with the eyes of a frightened mouse. "So this is the great man, the mental marvel!" thought Leslie. "Well, let us see for ourselves."

Taking a firm grip on his emotions, Leslie strode forward and greeted the visitor with a great smile and warm handshake.

"Welcome to Edmonton. I'm happy to greet you and we are all looking forward to your help."

The shriveled little doctor doffed his Homburg, whereupon his flowing hair popped up like that on a Japanese doll. He stepped back a pace, folded his hands over the handle of his umbrella and was silent for one split second before he smiled and said, "I doubt what you have just said, but I hope you will like me better by the time I leave, and I trust I will be able to help you."

Leslie told me later that he felt mentally naked, and hated me even more for foisting this introduction upon him.

On their way to the office where I was to meet Dr. Langsner, Leslie outlined our problem. Then, when the doctor indicated his awareness of our multiple murders, the detective began to question him.

"You seem to know about the crime," he admitted. "Please tell me about yourself."

Dr. Langsner looked straight ahead. Even when the police car swerved around corners, his gaze was fixed as if he were in a trance. In an accent that sounded more English than Austrian, he replied:

"I was born in Vienna in 1893. Vienna was very lovely and very gay. The university there was full of vibrant thinkers and it was my good fortune to study under the great Freud. I was there during World War I and watched the horrors of the 'shell-shocked' men. I became extremely interested in the mind and its functioning.

"Research took me to Sweden, but the pattern of study there was similar to that in Austria. So I went to India, where I found so much inexplicable intuitive control of the mind that I stayed until I had earned a very satisfactory degree as Doctor of Philosophy. That was back in 1926.

"Since then I have found that my knowledge is helpful in solving crimes. I don't use it very much because people are skeptical . . . just as you are. It is also not my desire to be a bloodhound; so I go only when I am invited or when I have a strong pull toward a case, as I did in Vancouver. But I guess you know about that."

Detective Leslie nodded a miserable yes. "What are you doing in our country?"

Dr. Langsner put his Homburg back on his head, leaving a lock of frantic hair dangling between his eyes.

Still he looked straight ahead, like a gyroscope that requires the entire world to revolve on its focus.

"My research here is a fascinating one," he said. "The minds of the Eskimos have been less touched, less indoctrinated, than those of any other group of people. The tribes of the Pacific Basin, the Micronesian and the Polynesian, have been corrupted by the white man. The natives of South America and Africa are difficult to reach for an old man such as I. So I have come here to study intuitive abilities of the Eskimo people. They sense weather changes; they recognize oncoming dangers; they use their minds with the same acuity I saw among the East Indians. I want to live with them and communicate with them through thought-channels. That is why I am here."

The wind was slack in Detective Leslie's sails. When the two men arrived at my office, Detective Leslie was walking respectfully behind the small figure of the doctor. It was a great sight to behold: Detective Leslie appearing like a shadow thrown up by a candle.

After cursory amenities, I gathered my sheaf of reports and set about to review the case in detail although I had the strange feeling that my conversation was extraneous.

"On July ninth of this year," I began, "the police station at Maxwell, some eighty miles from here, was notified by Dr. Heaslip that 'half the people at the Booher Ranch' had been murdered.

"Although it was 9:30, the summer night in the Arctic region was bright and glowing. Constable Olson drove the distance over the dusty bumpy roads from Maxwell to the Booher ranch house where Dr. Heaslip was waiting with Henry Booher, his younger son, Vernon, and a neighbor, Charles Stevenson.

"Henry Booher, a middle-aged man, led the way. It was as if a communion of silence had overcome them all, including Dr. Heaslip, the good country doctor who was accustomed to bringing life into the world and seeing it depart in a natural way. The four had been made speechless by the sights in the rooms ahead.

"In the dining room was Mrs. Booher with her head on the table as if asleep, but a second look showed the ugly neat holes of three bullets in her neck.

"You said 'half the family!' " said Constable Olson.

"Without a word, Mr. Booher led the way to the kitchen and pointed to another body—that of his older son, Fred. The corpse lay across the floor face up, having been thrown backward by the impact of a bullet through the mouth.

"Mr. Booher was obviously suffering from shock. He motioned Olson on and took him to the bunkhouse of the hired hand. He pointed once again—this time to the dead body of Gabriel Cromby, Austrian immigrant, who bore the unmistakable wounds of two shots in the head and one in the chest.

"Constable Olson was flabbergasted, and I am sure any of us would be, too. He was accustomed to such ordinary crimes as petty pilfering, stolen cattle and drunken brawls. Maxwell is a law-abiding community, by and large.

"But he did a good piece of work. He gathered everyone on the front porch for questioning.

" 'Who discovered the bodies?'

" 'I did,' Vernon said.

" 'What time was that?'

" 'About eight o'clock. I had been working in the fields for a couple of hours when I heard a sound like rifle shots. They seemed to come from the house. I came in to find out . . . and found mother!' His voice faded into a whisper . . . 'Then I saw Fred. When I ran to the bunkhouse for help I found Gabriel dead, too. It was awful . . . awful.'

" 'Then what did you do?'

" 'We have no phone so I ran to a neighbor and called Dr. Heaslip for help.'

" 'Is there any money missing?' asked the constable.

" 'No,' said Mr. Booher, 'nothing is missing. My wife's diamond ring was not even touched.'

"Suddenly, Vernon came to life. 'Where is Rosyk? It's strange we haven't seen him. Could he have done this thing?"

" 'Who is Rosyk?' asked the constable.

" 'Our other cowhand.'

"Immediately the anxious party set out for the barn behind which stood the small original bunkhouse of the

Booher farm. Rosyk was there all right . . . with two bullet holes in his head.

" 'And now there are four,' summarized Constable Olson. 'Two members of the family and two workers.' And turning to Henry Booher, he continued his questioning. 'Where were you at the time of all these shots? Seems to me you must have heard them.'

"Mr. Booher turned from the doorway where he had been staring out across his vast acreage. 'No,' he said, 'I wish to God I had heard them, but I was working up on the north part of the east section of our land. The sounds didn't carry that far.'

" 'And what about you, Mr. Stevenson? How did you happen to be here?'

" 'Henry stopped by and asked me to come over to see a new farm equipment catalogue. We have been thinking of purchasing a harvester together.'

"Mr. Booher nodded his agreement.

" 'Mr. Booher, do you have any idea who might be responsible for these murders?'

" 'No,' replied the farmer, 'we have no enemies that I know of. Rose, my wife, was beloved in our community for her good deeds. She has never failed to be there if there was illness or death.' His voice broke and he wiped his eyes with the roughened back of his hand.

"Constable Olson made the usual request that nothing be touched and instructed Dr. Heaslip to take Vernon and Mr. Booher to the Stevenson home. He then called our Edmonton office, and I sent Detective Leslie and Inspector Malcolm Longacre out to the farm. Want to take the story from there, Jim?"

Detective Leslie looked briefly uncomfortable and cast a nervous glance at the doctor, who was sitting stiffly in his chair with his hands still clasped over the gold knob of his umbrella.

"Inspector Longacre and I went through the routine steps," he began. "We took fingerprints all over the house and found later that they belonged to the Booher family and their farmhands. The murder weapon was a .303 rifle, but we could not find it. There was a .22 rifle and an old shotgun in the house, but neither had been fired for some time. One thing that interested us was the absence of rifle shells. The murderer or murderers had evidently carefully picked them up, with the exception of one that we found in a dishpan of water. That one shell, however, was of no value to us, since the soapy water had obliterated any fingerprint that might have been on it.

"The neighbors formed a posse and spread over the countryside in an attempt to find the man, or men, or at least the rifle, but to this date we are just as far from the solution of the crimes as we were when Constable Olson first called us."

I felt sorry for Leslie. He was obviously upset at having to make such an admission of defeat.

Dr. Langsner smiled sympathetically and leaned over his cane. "That is all right," he said. "Perhaps I can help in some small measure." Leslie smiled back. It looked to me as if a friendship between the two men was beginning.

That afternoon Dr. Langsner sat in on the inquest. We placed him at the press table and gave him the title of foreign correspondent. But trying to divert attention from the little Viennese with his wild white hair was a little like trying to hide Marilyn Monroe on Waikiki Beach. All eyes turned in his direction, but he slumped down in his chair and focused his eyes on the witness chair. He reminded me of a photographer adjusting his lens and getting his angle.

Later one of the pressmen confided that he had stolen a glimpse at Dr. Langsner's notes as testimony was given, and found, to his surprise, that the writing was not in English or German, but in an unfamiliar language that looked Oriental, perhaps Sanskrit.

By and large, testimony consisted of the facts I have already outlined, with a few new bits of information. One was the coroner's statement that Mrs. Booher was the first victim as she sat at the table cleaning strawberries. Fred was second and was probably killed when he startled the killer by entering the kitchen after he had heard the shots.

It was some thirty minutes later that Rosyk was killed in the bunkhouse, and a full two hours more before Cromby met his death.

Various neighbors and passersby corroborated the time

factor. The first three volleys had been heard around 6 P.M., the second after 6:30, and the third around eight. Since this is hunting country, no one had given the sounds a second thought.

A surprise witness, Councilman Robert Scott, introduced a new element when he claimed he had driven down the farm road around 6:30 and had stopped to talk with Vernon Booher. During their conversation, Rosyk had interrupted them by asking Vernon what chores were still to be done. Vernon instructed him to go to the barn and feed the pigs.

When Vernon was put on the stand, he was sharply questioned as to why he had not heard the shots. "As I have thought about that evening," he said, "it does seem to me that I heard shots earlier than eight o'clock, but paid no attention. I thought possibly they were a tractor backfiring, or someone taking shots at a killer fox that's been in our area. Stevenson, for instance, has sworn to get that animal." His testimony was concise and convincing.

When Mr. Stevenson was put on the stand, he seemed visibly nervous. When the question came, "Do you own a gun?" Stevenson fidgeted in his chair.

"Yes," he said, "but I don't have it now. And that's something that has bothered me, and I think I ought to tell you about it. My gun was a .303, just like the one that killed all those people. It was in my closet, but it isn't there now. Someone must have stolen it."

This statement caused a murmur in the courtroom, and the newspapermen wrote frantically. Dr. Langsner sat with his eyes focused through narrow slits.

"Do you have any idea when the gun was stolen?" was the next question.

"Yes," responded Mr. Stevenson. "The rifle was taken last Sunday while I was in church. It was there when I put on my meeting clothes and gone when I came home and took them off again."

"Why didn't you report the theft?"

"You know how it is in our country. Neighbors just come over and borrow things. We never lock our houses or bolt the barn doors. We don't think of things like city people do. If I needed a gun, I wouldn't think twice about borrowing Booher's, for instance."

Mr. Booher and Vernon nodded in assent. On cross examination, they both testified they were at church on the Sunday in question and knew nothing of the missing rifle.

At the end of the inquest, there was a gloomy meeting in my office. It appeared to Detective Leslie, Inspector Longacre and me that the questioning had brought out little new evidence.

"Seems to me," I said, "that three people could be guilty . . . Henry Booher, Vernon Booher, or Mr. Stevenson. No one of these appears to have any motive; so I am inclined to look for a madman, a psychoneurotic, bent on murder. I feel that our next move should be to search the countryside again for the rifle. There's been no rain, and fingerprints might still be visible. If we find the gun, we can check the files of criminals and people with mental records—and perhaps track down the killer. You note I said 'perhaps.' "

Turning to Dr. Langsner, I half-jokingly posed the question, "And who, in your mind, sir, is guilty?"

Dr. Langsner shook himself as if in a sort of waking sleep. With precise diction and clear voice, he sounded like an oracle:

"The rifle is unimportant. And there are not three suspects, but only one. The man who murdered all four persons is Vernon Booher."

Detective Leslie leaned forward. I tried to maintain my calm, but I confess I was a trifle excited.

"How can you be so sure?" I queried.

"And what proof do you have?" asked the legally minded Inspector Longacre.

Dr. Langsner looked at us helplessly. "Of course, I have no proof. I am sure, but I cannot tell you how I am sure. As I have told your distinguished police officials before, my conclusions are the results of electrical changes that take place in the brain. Some people, in fact most people, are not capable of this, but I am able to catch the brain waves. I was reading the thoughts of those who were on the stand today. Also yours, Detective Leslie," and he smiled a warm, friendly smile.

Jim Leslie looked embarrassed.

"Now wait a minute," interrupted Inspector Longacre. "Do you mean to sit there and tell us that you could read the minds of the witnesses while they were on the stand?"

"I do not know if I was 'reading their minds,' but I know what they were thinking about.

"When a man commits a violent and terrible crime, he overrides his instinct for decency and, at the same time, he is caught by the drive for survival. The criminal goes over the details time after time; he plans his excuses and develops his alibi. This is the reason for confessions. The persistence of thought drives him to vocalize his maldoings.

"The facts I learned from Vernon today are perhaps sketchy, but I can assure you, he is worried that you will come across a clue . . ."

"And that clue would be the rifle," I said triumphantly, still bent on finding the murder weapon. I was painfully aware that Dr. Langsner's suspicions, arrived at by telepathic means, would not hold up in any court, much less the punctilious Canadian ones.

"Why don't you tell us where to find the rifle?" I urged.

Dr. Langsner gave a little sigh. "Yes," he said, "I know where it is. While Mr. Stevenson was telling of its removal from his home, Vernon was, of course, thinking very intently about the weapon. I could see where he put it."

Dr. Langsner closed his eyes. "It is in a clump of prairie grass some two hundred yards back of the house. It is to the west because I can see the sun in that direction."

Inspector Longacre gasped and then, I feel sure, assured himself that the doctor had previously gained information as to the geographical site of the Booher home.

"If you take me to the farm, I think I can find it for you," continued Dr. Langsner. "But let us go tomorrow. I am very tired now."

Detective Leslie was on his feet the next moment and hustled his charge out of the room with the care and alacrity of a mother hen.

Noon the next day found the four of us together again on the Booher farm. It was clearly a large land-holding. The house was a comfortable two-story wood building. The large veranda was dotted with rocking chairs, and I could envision the Boohers as they entertained the neighbors on warm summer evenings. The equipment was modern, the barn newly painted, and the various farm buildings clustered under huge spreading linden trees.

I glanced at Dr. Langsner and inwardly chuckled at the sight. The mysterious little doctor was still carrying his umbrella in spite of the heat-filled blue sky. He was again wearing his black suit, and while his bangs of white hair were secured under his black hat, an unruly fringe curled coyly on the nape of his neck. Certainly the Booher farm had never before been graced by such a figure!

But if Dr. Langsner was uncomfortable because of the heat or aware that he was not dressed for the occasion, he gave no outward sign.

Instead he wandered aimlessly toward the back of the house. In my youth I remember seeing men with water witches, the twisted branches of willow which were held over the ground and which, they declared, pointed toward the best place to dig a well. Dr. Langsner, without the wand in hand, was behaving in somewhat the same manner.

We stood on the sidelines and watched.

After some twenty minutes of trancelike crisscrossing of steps, he returned to us, motioned to Leslie to follow, and took off like a greyhound after a rabbit. It was a sight to behold—the tall Leslie almost stepping on the heels of the little man in the Homburg.

The professor stopped suddenly between a linden tree on the left and a bunkhouse on the right. Leslie almost ran him down. The doctor's eyes were closed and he put his hand like a visor over them.

"Ja, ja! Ach Gott," he exclaimed, "I have it now. If you will walk straight ahead about ten large steps . . ."

Leslie began pacing off. On the ninth step he stumbled and almost fell. As he regained his balance, he fumbled and picked up a rifle with the satisfied and triumphant statement. "Here it is!"

"Oh, no," breathed Inspector Longacre, and it was hard to tell whether he was impressed or astonished. Likely it was both.

Detective Leslie carefully wrapped the rifle and we headed back to Edmonton's crime laboratory where the gun would be checked for fingerprints.

"You will not find any prints," warned Dr. Langsner. "Vernon wiped them off. He kept thinking how glad he was that he had taken that precaution."

At this point, then, none of us was surprised when the gun was found free of fingerprints.

Sufficiently impressed with the validity of Dr. Langsner's predictions, we did not want to take chances. I booked Vernon, not on suspicion of murder but as a material witness, and had him placed in one of the cells in the Edmonton jail "for his own protection."

"Let me tell you what we should do next," suggested Dr. Langsner.

We were more than ready to hear his opinion. Assuming Vernon was guilty, we had not one whit of proof, and no jury in the world would take "brain waves" as evidence. We were remembering the professor's demonstration on the Booher farm as well as his past record in the solution of crimes.

Following the doctor's suggestions, we placed a chair for him in front of Vernon's cell and issued orders that there was to be no unnecessary noise and no interruptions.

Dr. Langsner seated himself and leaned forward, staring at Vernon through the bars. Vernon's reactions vacillated from an attempt to be conversational to angry profanity until, at last, he sat on his cot with his back toward the doctor and maintained a stolid, defiant silence. And Dr. Langsner just sat and stared.

The entire episode required some sixty minutes. At the end of that time, Dr. Langsner smiled at Vernon's back and said a gay "Goodbye." We all went into the office.

"Vernon is definitely guilty. He killed his mother because he hated her, for some reason that I cannot quite get. He has no regret for shooting her, but he is sorry he killed his brother. When he went into the dining room to kill his mother, she spoke to him without turning around. It startled him, for he expected her to look at him. He fired, and then from fury he fired twice again.

"Fred heard the shots and came into the kitchen. Vernon knew he had to be killed.

"When he ran out to hide the gun, he saw Rosyk and Cromby in the fields. He was trying to get rid of the gun, but when he feared Rosyk had seen him, he killed him, too.

"Two hours later he decided Cromby must also go. The weight of his crimes was heavy on his shoulders, and, although he really liked Cromby, he felt he should be safe and eliminate all possible witnesses."

"Dr. Langsner!" I interjected. "At this point, I have no doubt that the things you are saying are true. But how can we prove it?"

"Find the woman he fears," was his quick reply.

Woman? There had been no woman in this case.

"I do not know her name. But Vernon stole the gun on Sunday from Mr. Stevenson. He sneaked out of church, took it and returned before the sermon was over. The woman who saw him leave was wearing a poke-bonnet. She has small, pixie-dark eyes and a heavy lantern-jaw. She sat in the pew next to the last and to the left of the center aisle. She glanced around and saw him leave and watched to see if he would return."

"Find that woman," I said to Leslie, who was on his feet and out the door before I had finished.

By noon the following day Leslie was back with the woman, Erma Higgins. She *was* a pixie-eyed, lantern-jawed female, the sort of spinster who knows everything that is going on at every church service, including the mild flirtations between the young men and women. Yes, she had seen Vernon leave and yes, she had seen him return.

By putting our heads together, we set up a scene for Vernon that would, I modestly say, challenge a London theatrical. I placed Erma Higgins in the center of the room, facing the door, with Dr. Langsner near her and also facing the door. I remained at my desk in the hope that my position would give an awesome authority to the meeting. Detective Leslie and Inspector Longacre took posts on either side of the door, and Vernon's chair was placed so as to face the professor and Miss Higgins.

Even the lines were rehearsed. When Vernon was shown in and seated, Miss Higgins said, "Vernon, I saw you leave the church the day Charlie's rifle was stolen."

Vernon looked at her and then stared at Dr. Langsner. The doctor stared him down.

"I know you did," he admitted miserably. "I know you did."

For a minute that seemed like an hour, the only sound in the room came from an old-fashioned wall clock with a thin brass pendulum. Then Vernon turned to me in desperation and fairly pleaded, "Let me confess. I killed them. Let me confess to you."

He broke into great sobs, sobs that seemed to come from somewhere in the region of his spinal column.

His confession need not be told here, for Dr. Langsner was correct in every detail. The only new thing we learned was the motive for the first murder, which ignited the following chain of killings.

Rose Booher, though deeply loved in the community, was, at the same time, a dominant person who held selfishly and tightly to her family of men. Vernon, the younger of the boys, had been her particular attachment.

When Vernon, young and romantic and emotional, had threatened to elope with an attractive blond daughter of an itinerant farm worker, Mrs. Booher had been stern in her "No," while Henry had laughed off the crisis as a teenage whim that would rapidly die. In her passionate effort to keep her son by her side, Rose Booher had had the poor judgment to apply some unattractive adjectives to the girl and to order her to leave the farm one Sunday afternoon when Vernon had brought her to visit.

Vernon's resentment kindled, burned and became the explosion that took four lives.

On April 26 of the following year Vernon Booher walked his last mile to the scaffold.

Months before, however, Detective Leslie and I took Dr. Langsner to the train leaving Edmonton. Our words of thanks were inadequate to express our appreciation. The small check we put in his pocket, against his wishes, was trivial in comparison to the job he had done for us.

As he stepped on board, his parting words to us were, "Gentlemen, no man can escape from his own thoughts. . . . And now, off to the Eskimos!"

Some time went by before Leslie placed a small news clipping on my desk. His face showed the mournful expression of one who has lost a hero. The clipping read, in part:

> Maximilian Langsner, Ph. D., University of Calcutta, was found dead today in a small hut on the outskirts of Fairbanks, Alaska. Dr. Langsner was known for his theory of brainwaves and was doing research on the subject at the time of his death.
>
> To his credit he had solved mysteries for the Shah of Persia, the King of Egypt and the British Government in Asia. His unusual capabilities had also led him to aid various police departments in the solution of difficult cases.

When I looked up from reading the article, I found that Detective Leslie had already left the room.

These identical twins on the West Coast have remarkable telepathic rapport; they suffer the same illnesses, though living 150 miles apart, and one "knows things"—without any explainable way of doing so.

WAS IT COINCIDENCE?

Vera Randall

I do not know precisely when I first became aware of a sixth sense but I'm sure it was when I was quite young. It is well-known that children have the capacity to accept the strange and unusual. My unusual experiences stem from the fact, or at least are connected with the fact, that I am an identical twin.

My twin sister and I have many times started to speak and say the same words. And many times we have said nothing and yet had thoughts pass between us that needed no words. When we told our parents about this, they gave us a simple explanation. "Two peas from a pod are bound to *think* alike," they said. But it was more than just *thinking* alike!

There seemed to be a physical relationship that was more difficult to explain. Often my sister would have a headache at the same time I had one. After many attempts at trying to convince our parents of the reality of such simultaneous phenomena, we simply gave up.

After I was married, I related some of these experiences to my husband. "I don't believe a word of it," he said. He is a teacher and considers himself a scientific thinker. "Pure coincidence," he said when my twin and I went shopping in cities miles apart and bought dresses or shoes alike. "Pure coincidence," he insisted.

My sister also married. For many years she lived 150 miles distant from us. It was extraordinary how many times we telephoned each other at exactly the same moment. Was it coincidence?

Was it coincidence that when I was in labor with each of my three children she telephoned me and said that she was having stomach pains at regular intervals, even before she knew I was in labor? She has never had a baby. That raises the question: how could she describe labor pains so accurately? Must there not have been some secret communication?

My husband said that it is quite common for men to have pains when their wives are in labor. Thus it is conceivable, he said, that twins could have sympathetic pains. But could my sister have had sympathetic pains *when she did not know I was in labor?*

Unable to convince my husband, I gave up. Then a strange thing happened.

On a cold February night I dreamed my husband and I were at the beach. I do not swim, and my husband, who loves to ride the waves, had given me his ring to hold. It was much too large for me, so I put it on my middle finger. In my dream I was sitting on a blanket on the sand and touched my finger to check on the ring. The ring was gone! I began searching around the blanket. Unable to find the ring, I began to cry. Startled, I sat up in bed.

Moonlight fell across our pillows and I could see John sleeping soundly. About three minutes passed. Then I saw him touch his finger. He jumped right out of bed.

"My ring," he yelled. "It's gone."

It was gone!

I told him what I had dreamed. Frantically he searched the covers and there lay the ring between the blankets!

"Explain that as a coincidence," I challenged him.

"Maybe I rubbed my finger and you were conscious of it," he said.

"No, dear. I was awake. And you had not moved at all."

My husband was still not quite willing to believe in a

sixth sense. But gradually he came to believe that I was "sensitive." We went to parties where there were many people I had never seen before. Yet I would know every person in the room. That, he said, was because I have a vivid imagination. But could imagination enable one to know exactly what someone says about him? It has happened that I have been reading or watching TV and suddenly become aware that someone is talking about me. Moreover, I know exactly what they say. To prove it to myself, I have telephoned the person and had the words verified which I had "imagined." This has happened again and again. I am convinced that this is something more than coincidence.

A few weeks ago my husband took our son, who is four years old, to Los Angeles for the weekend. It was Saturday night, and I went to bed early and read. At nine o'clock I thought I heard my son cry. His voice was clear and the cry was as if he were beside me. When they returned home, I asked my little boy if he had been a good boy and if he had cried. He said, "I was good and I didn't cry at all."

I thought no more about it until several days later when we were taking a drive. My husband remarked, "Johnny sure was a good boy. He cried only one time."

I asked when and what time. He said, "Saturday night about nine o'clock when I had given him a bath."

My husband had an explanation for that one. He said that I had asked him to bathe Johnny Saturday night. And in my unconscious mind I was aware that he was bathing him about that time. It was easy, he said, for me to think of him crying.

Well, how about the following?

Recently, I consulted my doctor about a large lump that had popped up on my right wrist. "Ganglion," he said, and telephoned a surgeon to make arrangements for me to have it removed.

At this time my twin and her husband were living in Los Angeles and I had not seen them for several months. I was washing dishes when suddenly I had the feeling that they were coming to visit us.

I said to my husband, "I had better go to the store

and get a ham for Willie and Ray. They're coming, you know."

Within five minutes we heard their car turn in the driveway.

My husband laughed and said he wished I knew which horses were coming in at the races.

They put their suitcases away and returned to the kitchen. I had just dried my hands and glanced at the growth on my wrist.

"Look at this," I said. At the same instant my sister held out her right hand. In the same location on her right wrist she had a ganglion. She had also been to her doctor the same day I had.

"Well, I'll be—" my husband said. "I just can't believe it."

"Explain it scientifically," I urged him.

He rubbed his chin as if a solution were forthcoming. "I don't know. I just don't know," he confessed. "But it *does* seem like more than just coincidence!"

Here is a "to whom it may concern" letter from Dale E. Hoyt, M.D., of National City, California, headed "Re: Vera Randall and Willie Hemphill."

"The above named is a pair of identical twins. Each of these ladies has a ganglion on the distal end of the radius, on her right hand. In each case, the ganglion is approximately the same size, in exactly the same location, and has been noted for approximately the same duration."

"Coincidence or — ?" I said to my husband.

A father lost in the North Woods, a son's desperate search, and a famous sensitive who "read" exactly what had happened to the father from a phone call during which none of the pertinent facts were given. The author has written and lectured widely on extrasensory perception; among his current books is How to Make ESP Work for You.

ONCE AGAIN, THOUGHTS THROUGH SPACE

Harold Sherman

IT was the early spring of 1939 when the events related here took place. At that time I was attempting to recover my health from the emotional and physical strain of experiments in long distance telepathy with Sir Hubert Wilkins, which were reported in my book, *Thoughts Through Space* (New York, 1942). As an aftermath, I had developed stomach ulcers, causing hemorrhages which might easily have taken my life.

Under these circumstances, I refrained from any protracted attempts at experimentation in extrasensory perception. Even so, for some months following the conclusion of the telepathic experiments with Wilkins (from the fall of 1937 to the spring of 1938), I found myself in such a sensitized condition that if I permitted myself to become too sympathetically interested in any person, friend or stranger, I suddenly became attuned to his subconscious. I felt, momentarily, as though I was that person, while a panoramic series of mental pictures, feelings and impressions rushed through my mind—apparently from his memory stream.

Those unbidden experiences were frightening. I doubt

if I would have had the temerity to undertake those regularly scheduled tests, had I known the toll they would take and the emotional and physical aftereffects that would result.

It has been my practice to proceed as knowingly as possible into the unknown, and to adhere strictly to conscious development of extrasensory powers. I have wanted to be aware, at all times, of what was taking place in consciousness, and to avoid any influences which might lead to trance or semiconscious states, where forces beyond my control might move in and take over. I have seen too many men and women who have trustfully or unwisely submitted to "psychic domination," and who have had great difficulty thereafter determining the verity of any impressions, let alone maintaining control and direction of their own minds.

The subconscious, once permitted to act on its own, is highly suggestive. It can be activated by imagination, fear, desire, lust for power, or ego satisfaction—and can reproduce all manner of seemingly evidential, inspirational material which can only be fabrication of one's own mind, partially drawn from the memory stream and fused with flashes of intuitive perception.

To get through into higher levels of consciousness where it is possible to make contact with intelligence and even entities outside one's own mental field requires the concentrative ability to penetrate the resistance of the lower centers of consciousness directly related to one's body and one's present external environment.

The March, 1939, issue of *Cosmopolitan* magazine carried the first mention of my experiments in long distance telepathy with Sir Hubert Wilkins, the Arctic explorer, in an article which provoked great interest throughout the world. It was written by Inez Haynes Irwin and entitled "Some Call It Extra-Sensory Perception." This article antedated by some three years the publication of the book, *Thoughts Through Space,* in which Wilkins and I told our stories, as sender and receiver. The book included my recorded impressions together with the check report from Sir Hubert's diary and the log of events that had occurred to him or members of his crew on the dates which coincided with my "extrasensory pick-ups."

But it was the publication of the *Cosmopolitan* article which was responsible for my unusual experience in March of 1939. At that time I was employed as editor of the *Savings Bank Journal,* with offices on East 42nd Street, New York. This particular day, I was reading page proofs and getting ready to send the magazine to press. My mind was intently focused on my editorial duties when the phone rang. I answered it in a routine manner still penciling in corrections on the printed matter before me.

The caller, to my surprise, was Thomas Garrett, well-known hypnotist, who had served the Air Force in helping relieve the emotional and mental blocks of fliers who had crash-landed or had other harrowing experiences in the air.

Mr. Garrett explained that he was phoning on behalf of a young man in his office, a Mr. Yellen, who had just learned that his father was lost in the Canadian North Woods. Mr. Yellen was leaving that afternoon by train to join a searching party.

"Mr. Yellen has read the article in *Cosmopolitan* about your telepathic experiments with Wilkins," Mr. Garrett said. "When he learned that I knew you, he asked me to get in touch to see if you might get some impressions as to what has happened to his father."

The suggestion was instantly repellent to me. I had already received a flood of mail from well-meaning men and women, requesting that I use such powers as I had developed for the purpose of locating lost relatives or lost valuables, or securing other information. Many believed I was a fortune teller, able to disclose the future, and still others begged me to contact their dear ones in the after life.

"Please tell Mr. Yellen that he doesn't realize what he is requesting," I said to Mr. Garrett. "Telepathy would not necessarily be involved in such an undertaking. It would be more like what is called clairvoyance, and I make no claim to be able to sense what is happening or has happened at a distance. Besides, Tom, I am not in the physical or mental mood to attempt any extrasensory assignment at present. I am still under par and nerve-exhausted from my previous experience. I appreciate Mr. Yellen's confidence in my being able to help him—but please tell him this is not possible. If I *should* try and fail, I would get no thanks for it."

Instead of relaying these comments to Mr. Yellen, Mr. Garrett said, "Harold, I understand how you feel, but my friend is very upset at the news of his father's disappearance. I'm sure it would make him feel better if he could at least talk to you. Would you let me put him on the phone, and explain to him yourself?"

More to save time than for any other reason, I said, "All right—put him on!"

Mr. Yellen, a man I had never seen, nor had even known existed until a few moments before, came on the phone. He was sincerely apologetic, said he hadn't meant to request anything that would be an imposition, that he didn't have any comprehension of what was involved in the getting of extrasensory impressions, but he was reaching out for help in my direction because of what he had read about me.

As I listened to his voice, I became sympathetically interested despite myself. I thought, "What if my own father were lost in the North Woods, as his father is? Wouldn't I be just as anxious to learn what had happened to him, through any source that might be helpful or worth investigating?"

The moment I let my mental guard down—it happened! In a way it is impossible to describe, the inner centers of my mind became activated. I began to see vivid mental pictures and to get strong, unmistakable feelings, just as I had when I had communicated with Wilkins. As these impressions came, I began talking.

"Just a minute," I broke in over the phone. "I am with your father now. I see him stagger out of the underbrush onto what looks like an abandoned Indian trail. He is in a nearly exhausted physical condition. He has not fallen into a lake or stream and been drowned, as some of the searching party think—but he is lost. I am following him, mentally, as he walks unsteadily along the trail. He goes about a mile and comes to a fork where the trail splits and goes off at right angles. I see him hesitate, undecided which fork to take. Then he starts off to the right and I get a good feeling in my solar plexus because I can see that, if he continues for about half a mile, he will come to a clearing where there is an old lumber camp, and there are two men there in charge of it, who can give him his bearings and help him get out of the forest.

"But now, I can see him stop, about halfway there, and turn back. I go with him as he retraces his steps to the fork, and now I get a terrible feeling in my solar plexus because I seem to sense that this fork is leading him farther and farther into the woods and that he has no hope of rescue there.

"I go along with your father for perhaps half a mile when he comes up against a great tree trunk which has fallen across the trail. It is so big and your father is so exhausted that he doesn't have the strength to climb over it, and the underbrush appears to be too thick to go around it. I see your father try again and again—and finally, I see him drop dead beside this tree trunk. . . ."

The moment I gave this impression, Mr. Yellen, whom I had all but forgotten, cried into the phone: "No, Mr. Sherman—don't tell me my father is *dead!*"

His voice broke whatever connection I had had and brought me back to a conscious recollection of what I had been recounting.

"Please disregard everything I have said," I urged Mr. Yellen. "I shouldn't have told you of my impressions, but they came to me so unexpectedly and so strongly that I felt impelled to speak them out. However, this could just be my imagination. There is no way of proving that your father is dead. Don't take my impression as evidence. I just permitted myself to get deeply interested in what may have happened to your father and this is what has come to my mind. However, it is probably all wrong and I would appreciate it if you keep these impressions to yourself. I don't want to get the reputation of giving out 'psychic readings' like this."

"I understand," Mr. Yellen replied, still considerably overwrought. He made an effort to calm himself, and then continued. "While you were talking, I made notes on the back of an envelope. If your impressions should be true, I'll let you know about them. Whether they are true or not—and I certainly hope my father isn't dead—I want to thank you for giving these impressions to me, for whatever they may be worth."

That night I told Mrs. Sherman of this experience.

"This mustn't happen again," I said to her. "I've got to find some way to protect myself. Imagine my giving a total stranger impressions over a telephone, just because I was suddenly gripped by strong feelings and saw certain scenes in my mind's eye! If these impressions are wrong and word gets around that I am attempting such psychic feats, it may well reflect upon the experimentation I have already done under scientifically observed conditions."

As the weeks passed and I had no word from Mr. Yellen, my conscious mind plagued me with the growing suspicion that the impressions I had given him might have been entirely wrong. I rebuked myself again and again for having expressed them to the very anxious young man.

The spring passed into summer and summer into fall. One evening, after I had given a talk on extrasensory perception at the Psychic Research Forum at the Hotel McAlpin in New York, two young men approached me. One of them, extending his hand, said: "Mr. Sherman, do you remember me?"

I meet many people in the course of a year, and I have an unusual memory for faces, but as I looked at this dark-haired, dark-eyed young man, I said, "I don't believe that I have ever met you before."

"That's right," he recalled. "But I have felt as though we have met—even though I only talked with you on the phone from Mr. Thomas Garrett's office. My name is Yellen."

Then, of course, the entire incident returned to my mind.

"Oh, yes," I said. "You are the man to whom I related an impression about his father, lost in the North Woods of Canada. I have always regretted doing that. . . . What *really* happened?"

"That's what I've come to tell you," said Mr. Yellen. "I took the train for Canada that afternoon after I talked with you, and joined the searching party. We roamed the woods for ten days and could not find a trace of my father, so I returned to the States and my job in New

Jersey. There had been new snows and it was impossible to get through in some places. This summer, I got a wire that my father's body had been found. I returned to Canada and went to the spot. Mr. Sherman, I walked along the abandoned Indian trail you told me about. I stood at the fork in the trail. I went up to the clearing and saw the old lumber camp where the two men had been, just as you described. And then I retraced my steps and went up to the other fork and stood beside the great fallen tree trunk, at the place where my father's body had been discovered. I came back to the States, intent on getting in touch with you, and telling you that your impressions had been correct. I went to see Mr. Garrett, only to find that his office was closed and he had gone South. Not knowing how to reach you, I decided to wait until either Mr. Garrett returned, or I ran into someone who knew where you were. The other night, this friend of mine"—and he introduced me to the young man accompanying him—"told me he was going into New York, to the Psychic Research Forum, to hear a talk by Harold Sherman. I said to him, 'That's the man I've been wanting to see for some months. I'm going with you' . . . and here I am!"

It is impossible to convey the mental and emotional relief that came over me when I received this confirmation of the information I had passed along. This had also been true during my experiments in long distance telepathy with Sir Hubert Wilkins. Since the receiving of impressions is a function of the subconscious mind, and since the conscious mind has nothing directly to do with reception, it will always put up an argument, after receiving in turn the impressions from the subconscious—insisting that they could not be genuine—that they have simply been figments of the imagination, products of wishful thinking, or of fear or worry thoughts.

Once the *feeling* of conviction that accompanies the receiving of a genuine impression has departed, one is left with the "doubting Thomas" of the conscious mind to plague himself. Personally, I have never been certain of an impression unless it has been "grounded" in my solar plexus. I apparently perceive it in the area of the brain or mind, but unless I get a positive "feeling reaction" at the same time, in my "second brain" or solar plexus region, the impression lacks conviction and may well be an intrusion of my imagination.

Control of the imaginative faculty is imperative to anyone who would develop his extrasensory perceptive powers. Because my profession has been that of writing, I am well acquainted with the feeling in consciousness when I am using my imagination. The feeling in the mind when exercising extrasensory faculties is distinctly different and can be isolated.

Even so, at any moment, unless control is maintained, the imagination or your fear, or worry, or wishful-thinking urges may enter in—and change or distort the mental pictures you may be receiving from the mind of another, or clairvoyantly sensing.

In the case of Mr. Yellen and his missing father, I cannot explain how my mind, once centered upon this situation, brought me the knowledge of what had happened. Nevertheless, I have found that, if one has a strong desire to ascertain some information about a person, whether that person is present or at a distance, the mind has ways of putting you in touch with many of the facts you are seeking.

It may be possible that my mind first attuned itself to Mr. Yellen's mind. Could he have telepathically received, through his subconscious, the record of what had happened to his father, direct from his parent, even though he did not possess the ability to pull this knowledge through into his conscious mind? Could I, then, simply have taken this information from his subconscious?

Or could my mind, in some electromagnetic manner still not understood, have used his mind as a trunk line, and made contact with the thoughts his father had left behind? Certainly I had to get this information from some source! Had his father been dead before these impressions had come to me? I had no inner feeling that I was in touch with a discarnate entity—even though I had a sense of being with the father as he was going through his last tortured experience on earth.

We have the evidence that my mind picked up these impressions. I have in my files a letter from Mr. Garrett, who was told these impressions by Mr. Yellen at the time, testifying to their authenticity.

Since the time that this experience occurred, I have done more private testing along similar lines, and have been astounded at some of the results achieved. I have come to the conclusion that, when you have learned to make your body completely relaxed, your mind receptive, and have been able to turn the attention of your conscious mind inward to focus upon what you may have chosen for a point of concentration—such as a visualized blank, white, motion picture screen—and when you suggest to your extrasensory faculties that they determine for you what has happened to such and such a person in such and such a place—*if* you can hold yourself in a state of absolute receptivity, maintaining an inner feeling of high expectancy, without forcing—*then,* in some indefinable but demonstrable way, attunement with some source of knowledge is made, and flashing mental pictures and strong feelings occur, bringing you the facts you seek, in whole or fragmentary form!

It is my conviction that we will, one day, discover that we are all connected, in an electromagnetic way, with the subconscious minds of all human creatures; that we all exist in what might be termed, for want of a better expression, a "mental ether"; that we are ordinarily insulated from the direct influence or trespassing of any minds upon our own; but that, under sufficiently emotionally charged conditions, we are sending and receiving mental impressions which may or may not get through to the attention and recognition of our conscious minds.

At present, all investigators are but "pin-prickers" on the surface of a vast mental field awaiting exploration. At present we are dealing with rather insignificant experiences of man—for instance, the plight of one man who became lost in the woods. However, this is a case of a man who left a record of everything he did behind, and a person who has developed higher powers of sensitivity may occasionally sense such happenings and reliably report them.

This is astonishing enough in itself, but I am far more interested in finding the meaning and in developing the control and direction of our minds which would enable us to realize our oneness and mutual interdependence, without which knowledge the great powers we possess within us may never be put to use on this earth.

A wife dreams the precise circumstances of her husband's death in Augusta, Georgia, when several hundred miles away, not in touch with him, and consciously believing him to be in good health.

"I DREAMT MY HUSBAND'S DEATH"

Benita Rivers

IN the first week of May, 1931, my husband Wilson Rivers went on a business trip to Augusta, Georgia, several hundred miles away from our home. While he was away, my mother and I were staying with my brother, Lyman Rhodes, and his wife at their home in Spartanburg, North Carolina.

Early on the morning of May 3, I was awakened when I heard my brother getting up and preparing to leave for his office. I lay awake for a while, thinking of my husband and wondering why I hadn't heard from him the day before, for it was his custom to write to me every day while he was away. I went back to sleep after a few minutes and had a most amazing dream.

In this dream I saw my husband lying unconscious in a hospital, bloody fluid pouring from his mouth. Five doctors were standing around him, expressions of concern and perplexity on their faces. They were discussing my husband. One of them said, "We have done all we can for him. Since we do not know what his trouble is, we know nothing else to do for him."

I awoke with a start, alarmed and frightened. I told my mother of my dream, and she tried to comfort me by saying that dreams "come by contraries," and that my husband had been too busy to write.

Later, while we were at the breakfast table, I received a telegram from the doctor in charge of the Veterans Hospital in Augusta. It read:

YOUR HUSBAND VERY ILL. ADVISE YOU COME AT ONCE.

I thought of the dream I had had just an hour or so before, and I wondered with apprehension what was its significance. My brother was called home from his office, and as he and I were leaving for Augusta I told my mother I was convinced I would never see my husband alive again.

When we arrived at the hospital and I asked to see my husband I was directed to the office of the doctor who had wired me. I went to his office, and this is what he told me:

"I am sorry to have to tell you that your husband died about twenty minutes ago. I want you to know that everything possible was done for him. We did everything we knew to do. He was brought to us unconscious, a bloody fluid coming from his mouth. He never regained consciousness. Five doctors, including myself, tried to save his life—but we could not diagnose his case correctly. We want your permission to hold an autopsy to determine the cause of his death. Perhaps this will enable us to save other lives."

This time I was awake. But the scene the doctor described to me and the words he was saying were the same I had seen and heard in my true clairvoyant dream.

I add here two statements testifying to the truth of the events I have related: one from my sister-in-law, Mrs. Jennie Rhodes Godfrey of Charleston, South Carolina, and one from my husband's sister, Mrs. Willie Rivers Young of Fairfax, South Carolina.

September 7, 1955

This is to state that my sister-in-law, Benita Rivers, told me of her dream as she related it in her notes, "A Clairvoyant Dream," before going to the hospital where she found her husband, Wilson Rivers, dead. According to the doctor in charge of the Veterans Hospital where he had been admitted, he had died under conditions almost identical to the dream she had had the night before.

(Mrs.) Jennie Rhodes Godfrey
Charleston, S.C.

September 9, 1955

I am the sister of Wilson Rivers, deceased, whose wife was Benita Rivers. I do declare that Benita Rivers told me of her dream before going to the Veterans Hospital in Augusta, Georgia, where my brother died. She said she dreamed of seeing my brother on an operating table, that bloody water was pouring out of his mouth, and five doctors were standing beside him and one had said they did not know what was the matter with her husband and that they had done all they knew to do for him.

I know that he had died as she had seen him in her dream, because my husband, George Young, also reached the hospital after he died, and with Benita Rivers gave consent to the autopsy that the doctors wished to make to determine what he died of.

The doctor told my husband of his condition and treatment before he died, which were the same as Benita Rivers' dream as related to me.

(Mrs.) Willie Rivers Young
Fairfax, S.C.

Mark Twain feared they would call his discovery of "mental telegraphy" a joke and waited many years to tell of his belief in the phenomenon, and of his own personal experiences with it. Mr. Munson is a member of the faculty of the Wesleyan Center for Advanced Studies.

MARK TWAIN'S DISCOVERY OF TELEPATHY

Gorham Munson

"All his life," wrote Van Wyck Brooks in his influential *Ordeal of Mark Twain,* "Mark Twain was attended by what Mr. [Albert Bigelow] Paine calls 'psychic evidence'; he never fails to note the marvellous coincidences of which he is the subject; he is always being struck by some manifestation of 'mental telegraphy'—he invented the phrase; strange phenomena of nature rise up in his path." And what did Mr. Brooks make of Mark Twain's interest in telepathy and psychical research? He did not take it seriously, which is what Mark Twain expected would happen if he declared himself on such subjects. Brooks disposed of these interests by finding them examples of "that boundless comic impudence of Mark Twain"; he accused Mark Twain of "childlike self-magnification, combined with an instinctive trust in luck."

Mark Twain had written about "mental telegraphy" as early as 1878. He had intended to publish the piece in *A Tramp Abroad* but removed it from the manuscript, "for I feared that the public would treat the thing as a joke and throw it aside, whereas I was in earnest." In 1920 Mr. Brooks threw it aside not as a joke but as a symptom of "essential self-ignorance."

I suggest that it it time—eighty-three years after Mark Twain penned his thoughts on "mental telegraphy"—that the biographers and critics of this great author do him the courtesy of meeting his simple, modest desire about this early essay; all he asked was that "the public should receive the thing seriously, and be willing to stop and give it some fair degree of attention." That's all—"give it some fair degree of attention."

By thc time he got around to actually publishing his "mental telegraphy" papers, Mark Twain felt that he had received convincing corroboration of his discovery. Mental telegraphy, he said, "is the same thing around the outer edges of which the Psychical Society of England began to group (and play with) four or five years ago, and which they named 'Telepathy.' Within the last two or three years they have penetrated toward the heart of the matter, however, and have found out that mind can act upon mind in a quite detailed and elaborate way over vast stretches of land and water. And they have succeeded in doing, by their great credit and influence, what I could never have done—they have convinced the world that mental telegraphy is not a jest, but a fact, and it is a thing not rare, but exceedingly common. They have done our age a service—and a very great service, I think."

It is exceedingly interesting to know something about Mark Twain that is not generally known, and that is that he was a member of the Society for Psychical Research from 1885 to 1903. This society had been formed in London in 1882, after William F. Barrett, professor of physics in the Royal College of Science, Dublin, had called a conference to consider the application of more scientific methods to the study of all types of psychical phenomena. Mark Twain was thus an early member, for he wrote from Hartford, Connecticut, in October, 1884, to accept membership in the pioneering society. His letter of acceptance was published in the *Journal of the Society for Psychical Research,* Vol. 1, 1884-1885, and is here reproduced in full.

Mark Twain On Thought-Transference

The following characteristic letter from Mr. S. L. Clemens (Mark Twain) will, doubtless, entertain many of our readers.—Ed.

Hartford, Conn., *October 4th,* 1884.

DEAR SIR—I should be very glad indeed to be made a Member of the Society for Psychical Research; for Thought-transference, as you call it, or mental telegraphy as I have been in habit of calling it, has been a very strong interest with me for the past nine or ten years. I have grown so accustomed to considering that all my powerful impulses come to me from somebody else, that I often feel like a mere amanuensis when I sit down to write a letter under the coercion of a strong impulse: I consider that that other person is supplying the thoughts to me, and that I am merely writing from dictation. And I consider that when that other person does not supply me with the thoughts, he has supplied me with the impulse, anyway: I never seem to have any impulses of my own. Still, maybe I get even by unconsciously furnishing other people with impulses.

I have reaped an advantage from these years of constant observation. For instance, when I am suddenly and strongly moved to write it—because I know that that other person is at that moment writing to tell me the thing I wanted to know,—I have moved him or he has moved me, I don't know which,—but anyway I don't need to write, and so I save my labour. Of course I sometimes act upon my impulse without stopping to think. My cigars come to me from 1,200 miles away. A few days ago,—September 30th,—it suddenly, and very warmly occurred to me that an order made three weeks ago for cigars had as yet, for some unaccountable reason, received no attention. I immediately telegraphed to inquire what the matter was. At least I wrote the telegram and was about to send it down town, when the thought occurred to me, "This isn't necessary, they are doing something about the cigars now—this impulse has travelled to me 1,200 miles in half a second."

As I finished writing the above sentence a servant intruded here to say, "The cigars have arrived, and we haven't any money downstairs to pay the expressage." This is October 4th,—you see how serene my confidence was. The *bill* for the cigars arrived October 2nd, dated *September* 30*th*—I knew perfectly well they were doing something about the cigars that day, or I shouldn't have had that strong impulse to wire an inquiry.

So, by depending upon the trustworthiness of the *mental* telegraph, and refraining from using the electric one, I saved 50 cents—for the poor. [I am the poor.]

Companion instances to this have happened in my experience so frequently in the past nine years, that I could pour them out upon you to utter weariness. I have been saved the writing of many and many a letter by refusing to obey these strong impulses. I always knew the other fellow was sitting down to write when I got the impulse—so what could be the sense in both of us writing the same thing? People are always marvelling because their letters "cross" each other. If they would but squelch the impulse to write, there would not be any crossing, because only the other fellow would write. I am politely making an exception in your case; you have mentally telegraphed me to write, possibly, and I sit down at once and do it, without any shirking.

I began a chapter upon "Mental Telegraphy" in May, 1878, and added a paragraph to it now and then during two or three years; but I have never published it, because I judged that people would only laugh at it and think I was joking. I long ago decided to not publish it at all; but I have the old MS. by me yet, and I notice one thought in it which may be worth mentioning—to this effect: In my own case it has often been demonstrated that people can have crystal-clear mental communication with each other over vast distances. Doubtless to be able to do this the two minds have to be in a peculiarly favourable condition for the moment. Very well, then, why shouldn't some scientist find it possible to invent a way to *create* this condition of *rapport* between two minds, at will? Then we should drop the slow and cumbersome telephone and say, "Connect me with the brain of the chief of police at Peking." We shouldn't need to know the man's language; we should communicate by thought only, and say in a couple of minutes what couldn't be inflated into words in an hour and a half. Telephones, telegraphs and words are too slow for this age; we must get something that is faster.—Truly yours,

S. L. CLEMENS

P.S.—I do not mark this "private," there being nothing furtive about it or any misstatements in it. I wish you could have given me a call. It would have been a most welcome pleasure to me.

This letter is entertaining, as the Editor of the *Journal* says. Mark Twain evidently felt that he could take a light tone with a sympathetic audience, but he wrote earnestly to the unconverted, as we shall see. In volume two of the posthumously published *Mark Twain's Autobiography,* he made an entry, dated March 21, 1906, that "certainly mental telegraphy is an industry which is always silently at work—oftener than otherwise, perhaps, when we are not suspecting that it is affecting our thought." He goes on to tell how he had been planning an article about Dr. John Brown of Edinburgh and had begun it the day before. "To-day comes a letter from his son Jock, from whom I had not previously heard for a good many years." He gave his reasons for thinking that Jock's mind had telegraphed his thoughts across the Atlantic to him, and concludes as he had often done before, "I imagine that we get most of our thoughts out of somebody else's head, by mental telegraphy—and not always out of the heads of the acquaintances, but, in the majority of cases, out of the heads of strangers; strangers far removed—Chinamen, Hindus, and all manner of remote foreigners whose language we should not be able to understand, but whose thoughts we can read without difficulty."

This, so far as I know, was Mark Twain's final word on telepathy. His official biographer, Albert Bigelow Paine, had noted that "psychic theories and phenomena always attracted Mark Twain. In thought transference, especially, he had a frank interest—an interest awakened and kept alive by certain phenomena—psychic manifestations we call them now. In his association with Mrs. Clemens it not infrequently happened that one spoke the other's thought, or perhaps a long, procrastinated letter to a friend would bring an answer as quickly as mailed; but these are things familiar to us all."

There was one time, though, when Mark Twain mentally telegraphed an error to his wife Livy. He told about it in a chapter entitled "I Send an Error by Telepathy" in *Following the Equator* (1899).

Mark, Livy, their daughter, and Mark's manager were lunching at Waitukurau in Australia. "I sat at the head of the table," Mark Twain wrote, "and could see the right-hand wall; the others had their backs to it. On that wall, at a good distance away, were a couple of framed pictures. I could not see them clearly, but from the groupings of the figures I fancied that they represented the killing of Napoleon III's son by the Zulus in South Africa. I broke into the conversation, which was about poetry and cabbage and art, and said to my wife:

" 'Do you remember when the news came to Paris—"

" 'Of the killing of the Prince?'

"(Those were the very words I had in my mind.)

" 'Yes, but what Prince?'

" 'Napoleon. Lulu.'

" 'What made you think of that?'

" 'I don't know.'

"There was no collusion. She had not seen the pictures, and they had not been mentioned. She ought to have thought of some *recent* news that came to Paris, for we were but seven months from there and had been living there a couple of years when we started on this trip; but instead of that she thought of an incident of our brief sojourn in Paris of sixteen years before.

"Here," Mark Twain concludes, "was a clear case of mental telegraphy; of mind transference. How do I know? Because I telegraphed an *error*. For it turned out that the pictures did not represent the killing of Lulu at all, nor anything connected with Lulu. She had to get the error from my head—it existed nowhere else."

Mark Twain tells the foregoing incident in a by-the-way manner in the course of a potboiling travelogue. But in two papers, "Mental Telegraphy," and "Mental Telegraphy Again" (written seventeen years after the first paper), which were collected in the volume entitled *Literary Essays* of the Author's Edition of Mark Twain's works, Mark Twain makes an impressive marshaling of the evidence supporting the case for telepathy. Remember that in this he was a pioneer; his notes on telepathy go back to 1878. He begins by saying that "another of those apparently trifling things has happened to me which puzzle all men every now and then, keep them thinking an hour or two, and leave their minds barren of explanation or solution at last." He was referring to the phenomenon of "crossed letters." "A few days ago I said: 'It must be that Frank Millet doesn't know we are in Germany, or he would have written long before this. I have been on the point of dropping him a line at least a dozen times during the last six weeks . . . But now I will write.' And so I did. I directed the letter to Paris, and thought, 'Now we shall hear from him before this letter is fifty miles from Heidelberg—it always happens so . . .'

"Yes, as I was saying, I had waited five or six weeks; then I wrote but three lines, because I felt and seemed to know that a letter from Millet would cross mine. And so it did. He wrote the same day that I wrote . . . In this letter Millet said he had been trying for six weeks to stumble upon somebody who knew my German address, and at last the idea had occurred to him that a letter sent to care of the embassy at Berlin might possibly find me. Maybe it was an 'accident' that he finally determined to write me at the same moment that I finally determined to write him but I think not."

Here is Mark Twain's commentary on "crossing letters." "We are always talking about letters 'crossing' each other, for that is one of the very commonest accidents of this life. We call it 'accident,' but perhaps we misname it. We have the instinct a dozen times a year that the letter we are writing is going to 'cross' the other person's letter; and if the reader will rack his memory a little he will recall the fact that this presentiment had strength enough to it to make him cut his letter down to a decided briefness, because it would be a waste of time to write a letter which was going to 'cross,' and hence be a useless letter. I think that in my experience this instinct has generally come to me in cases where I had put off my letter a good while in the hope that the other person would write."

In further commentary, Mark Twain said:

"With me the most irritating thing has been to wait a tedious time in a purely business matter, hoping that the other party will do the writing, and then sit down and do it myself, perfectly satisfied that that other man is sitting down at the same moment to write a letter which will 'cross' mine. And yet one must go on writing, just the same; because if you get up from your table and postpone, that other man will do the same thing, exactly as if you two were harnessed together like the Siamese twins, and must duplicate each other's movements."

Mark Twain then cited the case of the electrical repair man. A firm had done some work about his Hartford home but did not do it satisfactorily. When the bill arrived Mark Twain wrote back stating that he wanted the work perfected before he paid the bill. The firm pled that they were extremely busy but would send a man when able. More than two months passed. Then Twain sat down and wrote a letter of a page or so. At this point—it was in the evening—he had the feeling that the firm had begun to act. He cut his letter short, sealed it, and left it downstairs for the postman. When he came down to breakfast, however, he found that the postman had not yet called but the electrical repair man had been there, had done his work, and had left. It seems that he had received his orders the previous evening and had come up on the night train. "If that was an 'accident,' " Mark Twain remarked, "it took about three months to get it up in good shape."

The next example cited occurred when Mark Twain arrived in Washington, D.C., registered at the Arlington Hotel, and decided about ten o'clock in the evening to take a stroll. He knew that a friend, Mr. O., was in town and wished to find him but did not know where he was stopping. Toward midnight, Twain stepped into a cigar store, listened to drummers' talk for about fifteen minutes, and then made a prophecy to himself: he would go out the door, turn to the left, walk ten steps, and meet his friend. He did this and met his friend exactly as he had prophesied.

"That I should step out there and stumble upon Mr. O.—was nothing," Mark Twain commented, "but that I should know beforehand that I was going to do it was a good deal. It is a very curious thing when you come to look at it. I stood far within the cigar shop when I delivered my prophecy; I walked about five steps to the door, opened it, closed it after me, walked down a flight of three steps to the sidewalk, then turned to the left and walked four or five more, and found my man. I repeat that in itself the thing was nothing; but to know it would happen so *beforehand,* wasn't that really curious?"

Mark Twain passed on to matters of minor curiosity. "I have criticized absent people so often, and then discovered, to my humiliation, that I was talking with their relatives, that I have grown superstitious about that sort of thing and dropped it . . .

"We are always mentioning people, and in that very instant they appear before us. We laugh, and say, 'Speak of the devil,' and so forth, and there we drop it, considering it an 'accident.' It is a cheap and convenient way of disposing of a grave and very puzzling mystery. The fact is, it does seem to happen too often to be an accident."

The next example of thought-communication Mark Twain cited was probably the most startling to him. Paine wrote that it raised to a fever-point whatever interest in mental telegraphy Mark Twain may have had before. It was the case of William H. Wright, a journalist of Virginia City, Nevada, who wrote under the name of Dan de Quille. It suddenly occurred to Mark Twain that the time was ripe and the public ready for a book about the Nevada silver mines. The "Great Bonanza" was in the news. Casting about for an author for this timely book, Twain thought of William H. Wright, with whom he had worked as a reporter a dozen years previously. He drafted a letter to Wright on March 2, urging the project upon him and even outlining a book. Then the thought occurred to Twain that he would be in an uncomfortable position if Wright wrote the book at his suggestion and no publisher wanted it. He pigeonholed his letter and instead sent a note to Bliss, his own publisher, asking him to name a time for a business consultation, intending to press the project. But Bliss was out of town, the note remained unanswered, and the matter passed out of Twain's mind.

On the 9th of March, three or four letters arrived, and Twain noticed that one was from Wright. He said to a visiting relative: "Now I will do a miracle. I will tell you everything this letter contains—date, signature, and all—without breaking the seal. It is from a Mr. Wright, of Virginia City, Nevada, and is dated the second of March—seven days ago. Mr. Wright proposes to make a book about the silver mines and the 'Great Bonanza,' and asks what I, as a friend, think of the idea. He says his subjects are to be so and so, their order and sequence so and so, and he will close with a history of the chief feature of the book, the 'Great Bonanza'."

Mark Twain then opened the letter and showed that he had stated the date and the contents correctly. The letter contained what Twain's own unsent letter contained.

This was not clairvoyance, Twain remarked, inasmuch as he did not actually see the writing paranormally. Instead he seemed to know absolutely the contents of the letter in correct order and detail, but he had to word them himself. "I translated them, so to speak, out of Wright's language into my own. Wright's letter and the one which I had written to him and never sent were in substance the same."

Twain said that he could not doubt "that Mr. Wright's mind and mine had been in close and crystal-clear communication with each other across three thousand miles of mountain and desert on the morning of the 2nd of March. I did not consider that both minds *originated* that succession of ideas, but that one mind originated it, and simply telegraphed it to the other. I was curious to know which brain was the telegrapher and which the receiver, so I wrote and asked for particulars. Mr. Wright's reply showed that his mind had done the originating and telegraphing, and mine the receiving."

The incident had a happy sequel. William Wright (Dan de Quille) came to Hartford for an extended visit with Twain. He wrote *The Big Bonanza* there, and Bliss successfully published it a year later.

"Last spring," Mark Twain continued, "a literary friend of mine [William Dean Howells], who lived a hundred miles away, paid me a visit, and in the course of our talk he said he had made a discovery—conceived an entirely new idea—one which certainly had never been used in literature. He told me what it was. I handed him a manuscript, and said he would find substantially the same idea in that—a manuscript which I had written a week before. The idea had been in my mind since the previous November; it had only entered his while I was putting it on paper, a week gone by. He had not yet written his; so he left it unwritten, and gracefully made over all his right and title in the idea to me."

Mark Twain bolstered his case by introducing two newspaper clippings of literary coincidences, one relating to Howell's *Atlantic Monthly* story, "Dr. Breen's Practice," the other relating to Miss Alcott's novel, *Moods*. He recalled several poems whose authorship had been claimed by two or three at the same time, and said, somewhat rashly, "These were all blameless cases of unintentional and unwitting mental telegraphy, I judge." He capped his literary coincidences with a quotation from Boswell's *Johnson:* "Voltaire's *Candide* is wonderfully similar in its plan and conduct to Johnson's *Rasselas;* insomuch that I have heard Johnson say that if they had not been published so closely one after the other that there was no time for imitation, it would have been in vain to deny that the scheme of that which came latest was taken from the other."

Mark Twain stoutly declared his conclusion from the evidence he had presented. "I am forced to believe," he said firmly, "that one human mind (still inhabiting the flesh) can communicate with another, over any sort of a distance, and without any artificial preparation of 'sympathetic conditions' to act as a transmitting agent. I suppose that when the sympathetic conditions happen to exist the two minds communicate with each other, and that otherwise they don't; and I suppose that if the sympathetic conditions could be kept up right along, the two minds would continue to correspond without limit as to time.

"Now there is that curious thing which happens to everybody: suddenly a succession of thoughts or sensations flocks in upon you, which startles you with the weird idea that you have ages ago experienced just this succession of thoughts or sensations in a previous existence. The previous existence is possible, no doubt, but I am persuaded that the solution of this hoary mystery lies not there, but in the fact that some faroff stranger has been telegraphing his thoughts and sensations into your consciousness, and that he stopped because some countercurrent or other obstruction intruded and broke the line of communication. Perhaps they seem repetitious to you because they *are* repetitious, got at second hand from the other man. Possibly Mr. Brown, the 'mind-reader,' reads other people's minds, possibly he does not; but I know of a surety that I have read another man's mind, and therefore I do not see why Mr. Brown shouldn't do the like also."

Twain's brushing aside of Plato's doctrine of reminiscence is certainly the weakest paragraph in his paper on "Mental Telegraphy," but he recovers to the resounding affirmation: "I know of a surety that I have read another man's mind."

Three years after writing the first draft of this paper, Twain began tacking on additional thoughts and evidences to it. He claimed that "when I get tired of waiting upon a man whom I very much wish to hear from, I sit down and *compel* him to write, whether he wants to or not; that is to say, I sit down and write him, and then tear my letter up, satisfied that my act has forced him to write me at the same moment. I do not need to mail my letter—the writing it is the essential thing."

A second time Mark Twain performed for a visitor the miracle of correctly describing a letter's contents without opening the envelope. "It is from Mrs.——, and she says she was in New York last Saturday, and was proposing to run up here in the afternoon train and surprise us, but at the last minute, changed her mind and returned westward to her home."

Twain then opened the letter and the details were found exactly correct. He remarked that he had no suspicion that this lady was coming to New York, or that she had even a remote intention of visiting them.

The members of Mark's family, especially his wife Livy, as already illustrated in the extract from *Following the Equator,* often finished sentences or thoughts which Mark had begun to speak aloud. This family facility at completing his half-spoken thoughts was another reason why Mark Twain declared that "I think I *know* now that mind can communicate accurately with mind without the aid of the slow and clumsy vehicle of speech."

Why not an invention then to facilitate mental telegraphy? Mark called for the invention of the *phrenophone*: "a method whereby the communicating of mind with mind may be brought under command and reduced to certainty and system . . . Doubtless the something which conveys our thoughts through the air from brain to brain is a finer and subtler form of electricity, and all we need do is to find out how to capture it and how to force it to do its work, as we have had to do in the case of the electric currents."

Mark Twain had difficulty stopping once he was on the subject of mental telegraphy. He added a postscript to his paper in which he quoted what John Fiske, in the *Atlantic Monthly* for June, 1882, had had to say about the Darwin and Wallace "coincidence" in a theory of evolution. He introduced another newspaper clipping which told a highly amusing story about coincidences in the discovery of a greatly needed roll of wallpaper, and finally he wondered if, during your waking hours, "you can be asleep—at least, wholly unconscious—for a time, and not suspect that it has happened, and not have any way to prove that it *has* happened."

It's a good story as he tells it. He prefaces by saying that "ever since the English Society for Psychical Research began its investigations of ghost stories, haunted houses, and apparitions of the living and the dead, I have read their pamphlets with avidity as fast as they arrived."

Mark Twain saw a man coming up the walk to his house. He wished to avoid him—Twain was standing on his porch at the time—and he tried to look like a stranger himself. The man disappeared about twenty-five feet away and Twain was positive that he had seen an apparition. However, when he entered his house a few minutes later he was astounded to find the man waiting in the hallway. He had rung the bell and the colored servant had admitted him. What had happened? "During at least sixty seconds that day," Twain decided, "I was asleep, or at least totally unconscious, without suspecting it." This led him to conclude his postscript to his first paper on

"Mental Telegraphy" with these searching questions: "Now how are you to tell when you are awake? What have you to go by?"

Seventeen years later Mark Twain returned to the subject of "mental telegraphy" in a second paper, and he started it with an even better story of an apparition than the one just cited. He and George W. Cable were sharing the lecture platform on a Canadian tour, and in Montreal they were given a reception in the Windsor Hotel. They were stationed at one end of a long drawing room and greeted a throng of admirers who came in the opposite end, moved up in a line, shook hands and said a few words, and passed on. Mark Twain suddenly recognized a familiar face in the crowd and said to himself, "That is Mrs. R.; I had forgotten that she was a Canadian." He had known Mrs. R. in Carson City, Nevada, but he had not seen nor heard of her for twenty years. Nor had he been thinking about her and there had been nothing to suggest her to him. Nevertheless Twain knew her instantly and he noted some particulars of her dress. People continued to shake his hand but he managed to catch glimpses of Mrs. R. as she progressed with the slow-moving crowd across the room. He saw her start up the left-hand side and was able to take a full front view of her face. She came within twenty feet of him. But she never reached him. Twain, thinking that Mrs. R. must still be in the room and would finally come, was disappointed when the reception was over.

When Mark Twain arrived at the lecture hall that evening, he was told that there was somebody in the waiting room to see him. Mark Twain walked in and instantly recognized Mrs. R. in a group of about ten ladies. She was dressed exactly as she was when Twain had seen her at the reception. "I knew you the moment you appeared at the reception," he said to her, "and you were dressed precisely as you are now. When they told me a moment ago that I should find a friend in this room, your image rose before me, dress and all, just as I had seen you at the reception." But Mrs. R. had not attended the reception! At the time of the reception she had been on a train approaching Montreal. Mark Twain thought that she must have been thinking of him as she traveled toward him.

But Mark Twain's experience with the apparition of Mrs. R. is, as Raymond Bayless has observed in *The Journal of the American Society for Psychical Research* (April, 1960), "plainly far more complicated than the usual explanation of telepathy will cover. If it were not for the coincidence of the appearance of Mrs. R. and her subsequent arrival at the lecture hall, the entire matter could have been merely a matter of false recognition. However, the coincidence of the 'apparition' and the arrival of the actual person plus the fact that Mark Twain states that both were dressed identically, clearly indicates paranormality (especially when his additional examples are remembered) and point particularly to a form of 'astral' or ESP projection."

The rest of "Mental Telegraphy Again" is less impressive. Twain tells of a "letter crossing" incident in which he received a letter from an Australian lecture manager answering "the single essential detail of my letter [posted in Europe] three days after I had mailed my inquiry." Then there was the matter of his being made an honorary member of the Lotos Club about the time that he was lunching at the Century Club with an editor who told him he would suggest honorary membership at the Lotos Club. And finally Mark Twain tells an anecdote to his friend, the Reverend Joseph H. Twichell, as they are riding on the trolley car out to Farmington, near Hartford. Out there one of the young ladies of Miss Porter's school stepped forth from a party of school companions and said to Twain, "You don't remember me but you were introduced to me in the arcade in Milan two years and a half ago by Lieutenant H." The lieutenant had figured in the anecdote Mark Twain had been relating to Twichell.

"What had put that story into my head after all that stretch of time?" Twain wondered. "Was it just the proximity of that young girl, or was it merely an odd accident?"

Mark Twain had great confidence in his discovery of mental telegraphy. When at last he published his first paper on the subject, he crowed a little. "Now see how the world has moved since then. These small experiences of mine, which were too formidable at that time for admission to a grave magazine—if the magazine must allow them to appear as something above and beyond 'accidents' and 'coincidences'—are trifling and commonplace now, since the flood of light recently cast upon mental telegraphy by the intelligent labors of the Psychical Society [London]. But I think they are worth publishing, just to show what harmless and ordinary matters were considered dangerous and incredible eight or ten years ago."

And now see how the world has moved since Mark Twain penned the lines above. Today Mark Twain's observations and investigations into the paranormal are definitely rated as one of his many remarkable achievements. He is at last honored as a true pioneer in telepathy.

Awakened at night by a woman's voice, a Utah housewife did not at first suspect that it might be a cry from her mother—it did not come by phone—fifteen miles away.

CALL IN THE NIGHT

Velma Dorrity Cloward

In the winter of 1924, my husband and I and our three children were living on a ranch in Greenwood, Utah. On Christmas Day, we planned to visit my mother, who was ill and in the hospital at Fillmore, a small town fifteen miles away. But it was almost noon on that icy Christmas morning before I had milked the cows, cleaned the separator, and had the children dressed for their holiday visit. Finally, when we were ready to leave, we discovered that our Hereford bull was caught in a barbed-wire fence. My husband would have to attend to the animal—and I would have to drive the children to Fillmore in our horse-drawn sleigh over the snow-covered roads.

My husband suggested that he should remove our temperamental horse, Old Cal, from the harness, and put Blacky, a tamer creature, in his place.

"I hate to have you drive Old Cal," he said. "He'd kick your head off if anything went wrong and you got near his heels."

I protested that I was not afraid of Old Cal. After all, I had been around horses all my life, and had even broken them to saddle and harness. I knew that Cal was a beautiful creature with a treacherous kick. We had all learned to pass his stall on the run, for even in the stable he would pound the back of his stall with sharp, hard kicks. Nevertheless, I loved spirited animals and I respected this horse for his surefootedness on ice-slick roads.

Promising my husband that I would be careful, I seated the children in the sleigh and drove toward Fillmore. The day was heavily overcast and cold, but the drive was uneventful. I was pleased and surprised to find my mother so much better when we arrived at the hospital. Although she was suffering from an incurable illness, she sat up in bed to enjoy our company and the gifts we had brought her.

I had tried to keep my mother from learning that our excitable Cal was hitched to our sleigh. But my son blurted it out. "I think we had better go, Mommy," he said. "Daddy will be worried because you're driving Old Cal." After that, I had a difficult time convincing her I could handle the horse on the trip home.

"Supposing the doubletrees come loose?" she asked.

"They would just have to stay loose," I answered. "I promise you, no matter what happens, I won't get near Old Cal's heels."

"I'll worry all night," she said, "until I'm sure you're home safe." We kissed her good-bye, and I promised to visit her with my husband the following day. It was now almost dark as we started for home, and it had begun to snow again.

It was dark when we arrived home, and my husband had finished the chores. A neighbor from an adjoining ranch was there. He said that several of the men were going to play poker at Joe's—a bachelor who owned a ranch a quarter of a mile up the valley. The ranch men often spent an evening there.

I was very tired by now and wanted to go to bed early, so I told my husband to join the men at the card game. I was so relieved by my mother's improved condition that I was sure that I could sleep without worry. Although we knew that she could never recover, we had prayed that she would be comfortable and that the terrible pain would be eased. Today she had seemed like her old, happy self—at least until she had learned about my driving Old Cal.

I went to bed. From a deep sleep, I was awakened by

the sound of the wind. Then I heard a horse's hoofs loping up and stopping outside the ranch-house door. Someone called to me, "Velma, oh Velma!"

My eldest son shouted from his room, "There's Daddy!"

The call came again.

I thought I knew what had happened. Joe, who was a fine cook, often sent me a dish he had prepared. As I rose to answer the door, I was irritated that my husband had disturbed me to show me the food. I was almost at the door when I heard a third call. This time the voice was high and impatient, calling my name three times.

"Well, for gosh sakes, hold your horses," I said as I struck a match, lighting my lamp. I opened the door and looked outside. There was no one there. I saw nothing but the whirling snow.

"That's nice!" I said to my son, who was standing beside me. I looked at the clock. It was just 1:05 A.M. "Getting a person out of bed at his hour," I grumbled.

I left the light on and put some coal on the fire. But when I went back to bed, I could not sleep. I was waiting for my husband to come in from the barn, where I believed he had gone to bed down the horse for the night. Fifteen minutes passed, and my husband did not appear. Instead, my son came into my room to tell me that the call outside "didn't really sound like Daddy."

"It sounded like a woman. It was so high, like," he commented.

"He was just impatient," I replied.

I rose from bed again and sat with my son by the fire. We talked as we waited for my husband's return. But as another quarter-hour passed, I began to worry. My son expressed my own fear when he said, "I'm afraid Old Cal might have kicked him."

We dressed and went to the barn. An awful sense of foreboding had come over me. I was actually surprised to discover everything in order in the barn, and to see that Old Cal was eating contentedly. But my husband's horse was not there.

"He must have gone back to Joe's," I assured my son, but I could not explain why he would do so.

When we returned to the house, we discovered that

my husband had come home. Although I was relieved to see him safe, I was angry at his inconsiderate calling and disappearance.

"Where did you go?" I demanded.

"What do you mean?" he replied. "You know I went over to Joe's place. What are you doing up at this time of night? Is something wrong?"

We told him about the calls we had heard and the sound of the horse's hoofs. He was as much confused as I. Adding to our confusion was my son's insistence that the calls we heard were a woman's.

We were still discussing this when we saw the headlights of a car coming down our driveway—one very bright and one very dim light. This was the distinguishing mark of my brother's car.

"It's Bill," I said. I suddenly added, "Mother is dead."

I knew it just as if I had been there at her bedside. And I realized that my mother had been worrying about me and our dangerous horse when she died. Even before my brother told me, I knew that she had called me from her deathbed.

She had whispered my name only once, he said, but across the miles I had heard it six times, following the sound of horse's hoofs, at one in the morning. I could no longer doubt this when Bill told us that Mother had died suddenly, at 1:02 A.M.

Who would think of the caustic George Bernard Shaw as experiencing telepathic suggestion? Yet he wrote that such a "curse" had "damaged" him and a prominent New York psychoanalyst herein describes it. Among Dr. Ehrenwald's books is Telepathy and Medical Psychology.

G. B. S. ON TELEPATHY

Jan Ehrenwald

To an exile from Nazi-occupied Europe, England during the first years of World War II was more than a refuge. It was the experience of a people, sober and unemotional in ordinary circumstances, growing increasingly alarmed by the evil things closing in on them from the East. It was the sight of a nation which, to her own amazement, found herself fighting for her life with a furor not customarily attributed to the Anglo-Saxon temper.

But it also was the spectacle of men of science, of the arts, and of the medical profession, weary from a day's work in the laboratory, hospital or lecture room, snatching a few hours from extra duties with the Home Guard or Civil Defense so as to go on with their business of remaining rational human beings "as usual"—despite the cultural and intellectual blackout which had gradually been descending upon Western Man.

If the exile happened to be a psychiatrist he found a new and fascinating world of its own in the quiet premises of the Society for Psychical Research at 31 Tavistock Square, London. It was a time when the howling of sirens and the crashing of bombs had already broken the silence of the SPR Reading Room—"For members only." But it also was the time when Dr. S. G. Soal of the University of London and his associate, Mrs. K. M. Goldney, steadfastly refused to break off their card calling experiments with the champion sensitive Basil Shackleton.

It was a time when, regardless of blockbusters and Molotov cocktails, the soft-spoken Mr. Kenneth Richmond still seemed to have both patience and peace of mind to initiate a newcomer in the accomplishments of the SPR since the days of Frederick Myers, Edmond Guerney and Frank Podmore.

This is how I resolved to embark on a study of the principal data of psychical research from the psychiatric point of view. I did so even at the risk of my growing isolation from the ideas then prevailing among my more orthodox psychiatric confrères. A first step on this way was a chapter on *Telepathy and Primitive Mentality,* later included in my book *Telepathy and Medical Psychology* (Allen and Unwin, London, 1947). In it I tried to show that the concepts of magic and animism as described by Sir James Frazer were at bottom crude, prescientific attempts at coming to grips with a type of phenomena which since time immemorial seemed to defy the laws of nature as they were laid down by the protagonists of the scientific method.

To whom should an author, brought up in the austere discipline of modern neuropathology, turn for guidance in what was bound to become a conflict between his own scientific background and a vaguely perceived new science of the mind? His friends and associates had been scattered in all directions of the compass; his father had been dead for many years; a cruel turn of events had broken the bonds between his teachers in Prague and Vienna. Ties to new friends or figures in authority had not as yet been established. Whom could he ask for advice about the publication of his proposed book? For some inscrutable personal reasons George Bernard Shaw, the inveterate rebel, the sage and philosopher in a jester's disguise, seemed to be the logical answer. And so the first draft of a chapter on *Telepathy and Primitive Mentality,* accompanied by an appropriate covering letter, was sent by registered mail to Ayot St. Lawrence.

A week or so later the following letter, apparently typed by G. B. S. himself, was delivered to my house:

24th October 1941

Dear Dr. Ehrenwald,

I know of no way in which I can be of any service to you in the matter of your book. I am not a publisher; and it is waste of time to send MSS to anyone but a publisher. When publishers come to me they come for my own books, and to get nothing from me but a recommendation of someone else's books would infuriate them.

I have read the chapter you sent me. Nothing would induce me to read the rest because, being a very old man, and a contemporary of Fraser, I am completely tired of travellers' tales which are heaped up with the entirely unscientific object of smashing the Bible and getting rid of Jehovah. For me that sort of thing is out of date and unreadable. Your object is to establish a science of telepathy; but you have tried to do so by the Fraserian method, which has really nothing to do with it. The day before yesterday I suddenly asked my secretary, *a propos des bottes,* what had become of Maurice Baring and whether he was alive or dead. Nothing had occurred to remind me of him for years. Yesterday I received a letter from him. Apparently he, by writing a letter to me, reminded me of him before the letter arrived. This occurs so often that it may be worth enquiring whether there is not more in it than coincidence, though the number of coincidences must be enormous and the cases few.

Another experience of mine is more interesting. I spoke at a meeting in King's College in London. I was in perfect health and at the top of my form. I sat down amid hearty applause, very well satisfied with myself. Presently the meeting ended and I rose to go. To my amazement and consternation I found that something had happened to my spine—something blasting and blighting. I managed to conceal my condition and get home, but with great difficulty; and I remained in this state for a month, at the end of which, at the same hour, the blight ceased as suddenly as it had begun and left me again in perfect health.

There was only one way of accounting for this. I learnt that a lady who very strongly disapproved of me and who was intensely angered by certain personal references in my speech, had been sitting behind me on the platform. My spine was within point blank range of her face, which expressed concentrated hatred. Her curse damaged me as the curse of the Bishop of Rheims damaged the jackdaw who stole his ring. And possibly my recovery may have been due to the prayers of some of my friends. Anyhow it was a clear case of a telepathic curse.

I tell you all this because for me such cases are alive and interesting; but attempts to correlate them with Fraserian legends are intolerable. I can read Malinowski because he describes contemporary facts which sometimes suggest that Polynesians have more *savoir faire* than we have, and never bores me by hanging his facts on to worn-out fables.

That is why, I repeat, nothing can induce me to read any more of your book. And it does not matter a scrap, as my reading would not get you a step farther. I can only advise you to forget Fraser and write the book over again in the form of clinical lectures.

Faithfully
(signed: G. Bernard Shaw)

I have not been able to find a copy of my answer to Shaw's letter and I know of no reason to bemoan its loss. Yet there is one passage which deserves being brought back from oblivion because it had in turn elicited a reply from G. B. S. My letter acknowledged with due respect his advice and concluded with what I thought to be a perfectly legitimate inquiry as to whether or not there had been a *draft* in the lecture hall at Kings College where Shaw had suddenly been stricken by an attack of lumbago. A draft, I ventured to say, may have been a more plausible explanation of his affliction than black magic wrought by the lady with the evil eye. By return of mail the postman brought a postcard containing the following blast of four irate Shavian monosyllables:

There was no draft.

I can still see the irregular scrawl of his handwriting on the yellow paper—duplicating as it were, the sardonic wrinkles that mark the face of his portrait bust, sculptured by Lawrence Tompkins a few years back. Unfortunately, this precious card, too, has been lost in the course of my wanderings from country to country, from continent to continent, in the postwar years. But I have taken heed of G. B. S.'s advice—at least partly so.

Although failing to scrap the chapter which in 1947 appeared in my book *Telepathy and Medical Psychology,* I made a point of assembling my data in the form of clinical lectures as suggested by Shaw. The result is a second book devoted to the same subject, recently published under the title *New Dimensions of Deep Analysis,* (Grune and Stratton, New York, 1955). It is, among other things, an account of how I sought to solve a Doctor's Dilemma according to the prescription spelled out by G. B. S. more than ten years before the plan for such a book was conceived.

The story of a psychic from Edgewater, New Jersey, whose gifts have aided many actual police investigations and who overcame the prejudice of the Telephone Company against her ESP powers.

THE WOMAN WHO SOLVED CRIMES

Mabel Love

The taxi driver, becalmed in a New York traffic jam, fell to thinking about his own personal problems: should he sell his house in Bellerose, take that job in Detroit—things like that.

"Don't give up your job, son, your wife would not be happy out there," a hearty voice boomed from the back seat of his cab.

"What the—what goes on here?" Shaken, the driver turned to size up the smiling middleaged woman who seemed to have read his thoughts so accurately.

"You a mind reader, lady?"

"Something like that, only my gift is called extrasensory perception."

"Sounds like double talk to me," said the driver, wagging his head, "and if it's all the same to you, lady, I'll let you out at the next corner and you won't have to pay me a cent, either."

"Well, thanks for the ride, anyway," said his passenger as she backed out of the cab, more amused than chagrined by the ungallant dismissal.

The lady with the mental Geiger counter built in her skull was Florence Sternfels, nationally famous sensitive, whose powers have been recognized by a number of scientific bodies engaged in the study of psychic phenomena.

"I'm not a fortune teller, as some people seem to think," insisted Florence, as she was known professionally. "And I'm not a spiritualist medium, either; in fact, if I ever saw a real ghost I think I'd faint from sheer fright."

Certainly there was no suggestion of the mystic about this comfortable, motherly woman. She was held in high esteem by Chief of Police Edward Pickering and Mayor Henry Wissell of Edgewater, New Jersey, where she lived in a kind of storybook house overlooking the Hudson River. Her kindly deeds and rich chuckling laughter were familiar to almost everyone in the friendly little town.

The gift that Florence exercised was rare. She did not contact the spirits of the dead, nor did she predict the future by looking at cards or a crystal ball. What she did was called *psychometry,* and consisted of receiving impressions or messages from small inanimate objects. A pen, a piece of jewelry, a pocket knife, or any such object that belonged to the person in question, seems, with a few gifted persons, to arouse thoughts and knowledge about the owner of that object. Miraculous? Yes, it was. But did it work? A list of the problems she solved by this method will speak for itself.

Florence had been called in by police of other cities to assist in certain baffling investigations. Refusing to accept a fee, she explained, "As a good citizen I am glad to cooperate with these men who constantly risk their own lives to protect the public."

"It isn't always that the police are stumped when they call on me," said Florence. "Sometimes they just want to save the time that would be involved in a long drawn out investigation."

That's not the way grateful officials of York, Pennsylvania tell it in describing the assistance Florence once gave them in connection with a difficult murder case.

The crumpled body of an elderly woman had been discovered under a bridge, where it had been hidden after the victim had been strangled and robbed.

Identified by the police as Mary Jenkins, a person of orderly habits employed as a housekeeper, the victim had made it a rule on her day off to visit the bank where she deposited most of her weekly wages. Suspects in the case were Bingo Kane and his girl friend Sadie Tole. Kane, an unsavory character, spent much of his time hanging around a tap room where Sadie was employed as a barmaid. Sadie was known to be acquainted with the victim and familiar with her thrifty habits.

Their watertight alibi, accounting for their movements on the day of the murder, had made it impossible for the police to make an arrest.

Felix S. Bentzel, at that time Mayor of York, being familiar with her work, decided to send for Florence.

"First of all, I'm going to have a nice little chat with Sadie," Florence announced on arriving.

Detectives Farrell and Pinkerton, assigned to the case, agreed to wait outside while Florence confronted the glowering barmaid, whom the police had described as being "hard as flint."

"It will be a miracle if you get anything out of that tough baby," Florence was warned.

"Honest to God, I don't know a thing about it," Sadie protested at first, beginning to crack, however, as Florence, exerting the full force of her psychic powers, described every detail of the murder including a description of a third character who had not been previously linked with the crime.

"All right," Sadie finally admitted, "I went with two guys. It wasn't worth it, either, having to split $35 three ways."

With the guilty trio behind bars one hour later, Florence made her departure in the grand manner, after receiving a citation from Mayor Bentzel and a note of thanks from the entire police department.

Nor did the matter rest there. Mayor Bentzel wrote a warm letter of appreciation to Henry Wissell, Mayor of Edgewater, thanking him for recommending Florence and telling of her successful efforts in obtaining the confessions of the three.

Another police official who ranked high in Florence's regard was the chivalrous Captain George F. Richardson, former assistant chief of police of Philadelphia.

Requested by the police of a city in Pennsylvania to aid them in locating two missing boys who had run away from home, Florence had informed them that the boys could be found in Philadelphia, even naming the street.

With their faith in her prophetic powers dimmed by the discovery that no such street existed in the city, the weary police with good reason gave up their search and returned home in disgust.

Nettled by what she regarded as a challenge to her ability, Florence made a trip to Philadelphia at her own expense.

Arriving at City Hall she happened to run into Captain Richardson, to whom she related her tale of woe.

"That street name sounds familiar to me, may have been changed," remarked Captain Richardson. And so it had been, as a study of an earlier map revealed.

A car and police escort were placed at her disposal and Florence rode off in fine style in quest of the missing boys.

They were there, all right, and in a mood to return home, having all but exhausted their funds in a riotous round of movies, ice cream, hot dogs, and soda pop.

Florence's first psychic experience occurred when she was a child of eight years, living in Winston, New York.

On her way home from school, she liked to wander through an old cemetery, where she often copied names engraved on the tombstones in an effort to improve her writing.

One day, standing beside an unmarked grave, she wrote down the name Thomas Burns. Just then the old caretaker came hobbling down the path. "What are you doing, little girl?" he wanted to know.

"Practicing writing names," she told him.

"But there's no name on that grave."

"I know," faltered the frightened child, "it just came like a flash, Thomas Burns."

"That's the name, all right," grumbled the startled caretaker, "and now you get out of here and don't ever come back again."

As time went on Florence learned to keep silent about her psychic abilities.

At home it was different, with her understanding family of English stock who trace their ancestry back to Admiral

Horatio Lord Nelson, Great Britain's outstanding war hero of all time.

Incidentally, early records show that Lord Nelson's intellectual curiosity once led him to consult a West Indies seer who predicted accurately along with other pertinent information that he would reach the peak of his career at the age of forty.

If there had been any doubt in the minds of her parents it would have been dispelled by an incident which took place when Florence, as a teen-ager, foretold the loss of an uncle who lived in far off South Dakota.

"Your uncle is coming to visit us next week," her mother had said at the dinner table, but Florence's short-lived delight died as she suddenly stiffened in her chair, her eyes glazed as she stared into space.

"Uncle Ed is not coming," she pronounced her words in a dull, measured fashion. "He will never come here again."

Her words proved true with the arrival of a message announcing the death of her favorite uncle.

An early marriage and devotion to home and family did nothing to lessen the psychic experiences she made futile efforts to suppress.

Her flashes of thought from other people's minds continued to perplex her until she learned that this was nothing to fear.

The part Florence played in solving the mystery of the murder of the seven-year-old daughter of a Marine officer stationed at the United States Marine Base, Parris Island, South Carolina, was never officially recorded at the time it occurred during World War II.

Now it can be told as Colonel Arthur Burks, retired Marine, reveals the events connected with the kidnapping and brutal slaying of little Dolly Miller.

"Dolly was a great favorite with everyone," recalls Colonel Burks (then Major). She had the run of the barracks and it was unthinkable that any of the 17,000 men on the island would molest this little girl.

Word of her abduction was made known by an excited group of Dolly's playmates, who told of a strange man who had induced her to follow him into the woods with the promise of toys and a real live pony.

A searching party was immediately organized by Burks and the men were flung out in a skirmish line, covering a tortuous trail of copperhead-infested underbrush until ordered back to the barracks at 2 A.M. in order to get a few hours' sleep.

Burks, who was a close friend of the distraught father of the child, remained with him and a few civilian friends who continued the search all through the night. Among the most active of Miller's civilian friends was young Joe Keller who although just about exhausted, refused to rest or eat as he pushed on, shouting Dolly's name.

Standing in the eerie half-light of early morning beside the turgid swampland which surrounded most of the west side of the island, Burks suddenly recalled the suggestion he had received before starting out on the fruitless search.

"Get in touch with Florence," someone said. "Send some of the child's clothing to her so she may become in rapport with the situation, and since Florence has an affinity for metal be sure to include some thing, such as jewelry Dolly has worn, or if not available, then send in an old shoe with metal eyelets."

Burks, to whom the name Florence had no real meaning, was willing enough to grasp at any straw. Besides, his mind was receptive to the experiment since as a hobby on his own time he had been making a study of psychic research in his home.

Fearing the ridicule of his fellow officers he made quiet contact with Florence who agreed to cooperate provided she was requested to do so by some qualified official.

"I told her that I felt qualified to make the official request," Burks relates.

So, within a few minutes after receiving the air mailed package containing little Dolly's garments, Florence had made a map of the area where she said the body would be found, giving directions by air mail letter.

"I am certain," says Burks, "that Florence had never been there, yet we found Dolly's pitiful little body floating face down in the swamp, just where she said it would be."

Fearing his fellow officers would regard him as a crackpot, Burks had not mentioned his contacts with Florence, but now he felt forced to do so and to his surprise and relief learned that the Post Intelligence Officer and several others connected with the investigation were also interested in the study of paranormal psychology.

Weeks of intensive investigation followed with no clue to the identity of the murderer established. Burks, who is acclaimed as a brilliant writer of novels of adventure, science fiction, and factual accounts of travel adventure, admits that nothing he has ever written or known can parallel the mystery which continued to protect the fiend who had caused little Dolly's death.

"Once again I felt impelled to call on Florence for assistance," he recalls.

In the message he received from Florence shortly after the contact he had made by telephone, Burks learned to his great relief that the killer was not a Marine but a civilian who turned out in the best tradition to be Joe Keller, the active young man who had never ceased calling Dolly's name during the night of the hunt.

Florence's description of the murderer and his actions was so complete in every detail that he readily confessed and is now serving a sentence of life imprisonment.

A recent flash of the mind sent Florence on a trip outside the state, after a frantic husband enlisted her aid in an attempt to locate his missing wife.

"The police have been working on the case for over a week, and they finally suggested you might be able to help," the man told Florence. He said that the only thing to mar their happiness had been the agonizing pain of migraine headaches from which his wife suffered.

"She did say on the morning she disappeared that she was afraid that if she did not find relief she would have to end her life, but I did not really take it seriously," said the worried husband, "I was advised to bring some of her jewelry with me to help you establish rapport with her movements," he sheepishly said. "It sounds odd to me but see what you can do."

As Florence related it, she was seized with such a blinding headache she was almost unable to project her mind in the direction the woman had taken, as, crazed with pain, she had for three days wandered about.

"I get the name of a town," Florence said, naming a town that was miles away from the girl's home.

It was there they found her in the city morgue, where

her body had been taken by police after it had been recovered from the river. They had been unable to contact her family since she wore no identification of any kind.

"Tragedies such as this sometimes make me wish I had never been born with this strange gift," said Florence, who regarded her clairvoyant power as a mixed blessing which set her apart in a skeptical, sometimes even hostile world since childhood.

However, the late Dr. Hereward Carrington, director of the American Psychical Institute, who was engaged with other distinguished authorities in research on psychic phenomena, learned of her ability and contacted her with a request for permission to test her powers of precognition.

Dr. Carrington, an experienced psychic researcher with an impeccable reputation for integrity, had never been afraid to expose fraudulent practices in paranormal psychology.

However, he recognized and showed respect for Florence's psychic abilities after an extensive study over a period of several years. In his conclusions (reduced here to brief form) he said, "I am convinced that Florence is possessed of remarkable psychic abilities and of her complete honesty and sincerity."

The head of Metropolitan Detective Agency, Harry Levin, made an appointment with Florence for a client he described as a key witness involved in a pending murder trial.

Arriving that evening with his client and a couple of friends, Levin was gratified by Florence's success in supplying the needed information.

Just as they were about to leave Florence gave a cry of dismay.

"I see an accident. Please return to the city on a bus," she entreated the lawyer, but the men laughed uneasily and then were off, with Florence calling to them to be careful when they came to the bend near Fort Lee.

Minutes later their car collided with another. The lawyer was killed instantly as he attempted to jump from the car, although the others escaped unhurt.

On two occasions, following her appearance as a guest

on Jack Paar's and Long John's radio program featured on WOR, Florence was overwhelmed with visitors, who swarmed all over her lawn, telephoning and ringing her doorbell at all hours of the day and night until it got so she was unable even to eat a meal without being interrupted.

Mail arrived in enormous sacks; many of the letters requesting information also contained checks, money orders, and bills of varying denomination.

Living alone after the loss of her husband and only son and the marriage of her daughter, Florence sent for her brother Nelson, a retired businessman who cheerfully interrupted his travels to make his home with her as he took over the task of bringing order out of chaos, first of all returning all mail containing money.

His help was a godsend to Florence, who seemed to be as poor a businesswoman as she was a good psychic. Then anyone who wished to consult his sister on minor matters was obliged to make an appointment. Exceptions were allowed to attend an open meeting, where Florence served refreshments and attempted to solve the problems presented to her.

"She was never happier than when helping others," says Nelson, so they considered it well worth the trouble.

As an example of what sometimes occurred at these sessions, a young woman recently told of her father's loss of a thousand dollars he claimed had been taken from his bureau drawer that morning.

"Go home and tell your father to take his money to the bank first thing in the morning," she was advised. "Remind him he changed his hiding place yesterday."

"Human squirrels, that's what half the people are who come here with complaints of being robbed," laughed Florence.

About an hour later the daughter telephoned to say the money had been found in her father's tool box; he remembered having put it there because it had a stronger lock.

Of course, Florence could not solve every problem that was brought to her. Often her guests were forced to go away shaking their heads, as her hints shed no light on their particular dilemma. However, in the cases when she did hit the mark, the results were sometimes amazing. In one remarkable case she found some lost documents and incidentally earned kudos from one of the nation's largest business organizations, the Bell Telephone Company.

The telephone company, in an effort to protect their subscribers against any kind of fraudulent practice, does not permit listings of so-called psychics, and when Florence applied for such a listing in the New York and New Jersey directories her application was rejected.

Some time later, however, a worried official was advised to consult Florence with regard to a set of valuable documents which had disappeared from the files of the business office.

Although apparently skeptical, he agreed to contact Florence.

"I'll be at the office in less than an hour's time," she offered, and ten minutes after exploring the file cabinet which had contained the papers she succeeded in locating and restoring the folder.

As it turned out, they had not been stolen as had been thought, but had been placed by mistake in a collection of papers which had been stored in another building.

The payoff came when Florence reminded the grateful officials that the company had once refused to list her name with the designation of "psychic" in their directory. Convinced of her ability, they agreed to comply with this modest request, so she was finally listed in the Manhattan and North Jersey directories as "Florence, psychic," followed by her telephone number.

Attuned to a life full of magic meanings and messages, are the Australian aborigines very different from civilized man? This expert in ESP is convinced that psychic phenomena occur naturally and far more often among primitives. Mr. Rose is the author of Living Magic.

CRISIS TELEPATHY IN AUSTRALIA

Ronald Rose

In our inquiries into psychic phenomena underlying the magic of Australian aborigines, my wife and I have been impressed particularly by one feature. It is that the spontaneous experiences of ordinary aborigines (as distinct from witch doctors or "clever men") so closely resemble those of white people.

This, of course, is to be expected if the reported experiences of white people are genuine, and it is, indeed, collateral evidence for them. The aboriginal case material shows, too, that psi experience is modified or conditioned by culture, but that a basic pattern is apparent. In no aspect is the pattern clearer than in instances of crisis telepathy—where there is a paranormal knowledge of the sickness or death of a distant relative or friend.

The cases were collected in two main ways. At first, they were incidental to an experimental program of standarized ESP (extrasensory perception) and PK (psychokinesis; mind-over-matter") tests. Discussion of them with the aborigines concerned helped them to understand the nature of the tests and convinced them of our understanding of experiences which many of them believed to be peculiar to aborigines and never experienced by whites. In the aspect of the work with the aborigines, cases were specially collected. Natives were given a psi questionnaire. The first two questions of this were:

(1) Would you know if a relative some distance away died, had an accident, or was seriously ill?

(2) Has this ever happened to you?

The first question, it may be noted, asks for an expression of opinion or belief. Together with other questions of the same sort, it was used to give a rough measure of the degree of a subject's belief in psi phenomena.

Of all the subjects questioned, ranging from full-bloods to very light castes, from those who had at one time lived in a tribal state to those who did not even speak the native dialect, only three answered the first question in the negative! It was from the second question, of course, that accounts of crisis telepathy arose.

Almost every native at Woodenbong (New South Wales), where the bulk of the work was carried out, had himself had such an experience or, if he had not, could cite several who had. It was our very distinct impression that the experience is a rather more common one with aborigines than it is with white people.

What are some of the conditions likely to influence this uneven distribution favoring aborigines? The conditions favoring psi awareness are probably optimum in the case of the aborigines. Certainly they do not inhibit such experiences. The natives have a social inheritance of belief in magic—their search for casual explanation has, indeed, barely progressed beyond recourse to mysticism and magic. They are not merely ready to take note of and act on "psychic hunches," but, indeed, seek them. On the other hand, white people do not live in a psychic atmosphere so highly charged. Their outlook is rationalistic and, unless a psychic impulse is of an impelling character, they tend to push it aside as irrational. Frequently, perhaps, it never comes to consciousness, or is lost in the welter of sensory experiences impinging on the individual.

In some instances with white people the "psychic hunch" comes to the surface in crisis cases and it is in these that the elements common between the two cultures are clearly seen. First, there is an emotional link between the people concerned. This has long been recognized as a typical, but not essential, ingredient. The paranormal event manifests itself through what the British psychologist G.N.M. Tyrell has described as a "mediating vehicle," often an apparition. Less usually, a vague "feeling" is experienced. In the case of aborigines the system of totemic beliefs, which is part of their living mythology, is brought into play to mediate the information.

The mediating function of the totem is more pronounced in the case of natives who have once been tribal than with others. The native belief is that each is magically related to his totemic animal ("djurabels" or "barmyunbaie" in the Woodenbong district) and that members of the same totemic group have spiritual contact with each other through the totem.

Incidents concerning the death of one particular man, Billie Combo, who died last year, illustrate reasonably well the impact of the experience on differently related persons. That three natives had experiences concerned with the death of one man is itself interesting. Possibly there were others that we did not come across.

Billie Combo was a Gidabul (or Witherabul) native of about fifty who had been in a hospital at Kyogle (about fifty miles from Woodenbong) but who had left the hospital a few days prior to his death. As far as natives at Woodenbong knew he was in reasonably good health. He died suddenly following a heart attack. The three natives who stated that they had had some paranormal knowledge of Combo's death were all interviewed about a week after the event.

(a) Walter Page, a native of unusual intelligence, who has represented his people on the Aborigines Welfare Board, said that he was walking about the station at Woodenbong when he suddenly felt "dopey." He said that he had to go to his residence and rest and it was more than an hour before the feeling wore off. Page told his wife that something serious was wrong. He knew it was not to do with a close tribal relative or he would have seen in a vision his totemic rooster as he invariably does in such circumstances. His wife later went into the township where she learned of Combo's death the previous night. Although Combo was Page's first cousin he was not totemically related to him.

(b) Rene Robinson, an aged half-caste, said she was working in her cottage when she felt a "great sorrow" come over her. She knew that a member of her tribe had died, since this feeling invariably overcame her on such occasions, but she did not associate the feeling specifically with Billie Combo.

(c) Danny Sambo, a full-blood, alleged by other natives to be "clever" (i.e., a witch doctor) said that on the night of Combo's death, he heard a crow singing. This was the totem of both Combo and himself (and others, of course) and he immediately knew that Combo had died. He said there was no doubt about his feeling that it was Combo who had died and not another native. He had, as far as could be ascertained no other means of knowing of his relative's death.

These three cases range roughly from a vague feeling to complete conviction and in general this range of assurance coincides with tribal and totemic relationship. Where there is a totem manifestation, as an auditory or visual hallucination, the paranormal knowledge is most complete and the details of the experience most reliable—probably because the native is less psychically inhibited than others.

A number of natives have shown that they understand the hallucinatory nature of the totem manifestation. Walter Page, in discussing a number of experiences in which a totemic rooster had conveyed information to him of the death or illness of relatives, acknowledged that the bird heard on these occasions was not "real."

Bert Mercy and his wife Beatrice said they saw plovers circling over their hut during one night. Bert realized, he said, that there was something wrong. After a time he said to his wife, "I suppose old uncle's dead." His uncle had in fact died in Coff's Harbour (two hundred miles distant) that night, as they later learned. Plovers were his uncle's totem, Bert explained. He knew the plovers he and Beatrice had seen were not real but were "mind" birds. On the other hand, other natives have on several occasions claimed such animals or birds to be real.

Apparitions sometimes take the place of the totemic

vision or are associated with it. For example, Alec Vesper, a Bundulung native from Pretty Gully, was sitting one night with some friends in his hut. During the evening, which was still, they heard a stone fall on the roof. Vesper took this to be a sign of misfortune, since this type of warning had occured with him before. He could not tell precisely what the incident meant until later that night when he saw a vision of his sister, who worked in a nearby township. The apparition stood in the doorway of his hut, but did not speak. He said he immediately recognized that it was an apparition (he called it a "wogai," i.e., spirit) and knew his sister had died. She did in fact die that night, as he learned by telegram the next day.

Often to aborigines the conviction associated with a crisis case is so profound that it moves them to action. In his book *The Australian Aborigines,* Professor A. P. Elkin testifies to the assurance of aborigines following the receipt of apparently telepathic information.

"Many white folk, who have known their native employees well, give remarkable examples of the aborigines' power for knowing what is happening at a distance, even hundreds of miles away," writes Professor Elkin. "A man may be away with his employer on a big stock trip, and will suddenly announce one day that his father is dead, that his wife has given birth to a child, or that there is some trouble in his own country. He is so sure of his facts that he would return at once if he could, and the strange thing is, as these employers ascertained later, the aborigine was quite correct; but how he could have known they do not understand, for there was no means of communication whatever, and he had been away from his own people for weeks and even months."

The certainty that may move a man to action occurs not only with tribal people but is relatively common in areas where the tribe has long since broken down.

A Minyung (Queensland) fullblood, Frank Mitchell, for example, in the space of a couple of weeks, had two such experiences. On the first occasion he and his wife heard the falterting footsteps of his deceased mother on the veranda of their residence one night. Frank interpreted this visitation as a sign of death and on the following morning told the station manager at Woodenbong that his son, Billie, who was in Kyogle Hospital (forty miles distant), had died during the night. A telephone call confirmed his fears.

This case in itself is not particularly convincing since the son was in hospital, but it was followed shortly afterwards by another. Frank one evening called at the manager's residence for permission to leave the settlement. When asked to give the reason he said that his brother in Brisbane (one hundred miles north) was seriously ill and would not last the night out. There was no normal means by which he could have acquired such information, nor did he knew that his brother was ill. He left the station that evening by bus and arrived in Brisbane shortly after his brother died.

As with white people, aborigines also have paranormal information mediated through dreams. Often the dream symbolism involves totemic or pseudo-totemic significance. Such dreams also are remarkable for their clarity and vividness of detail. The two cases following illustrate the form these experiences sometimes take.

In each case the informant was Owen Anderson, an intelligent caste native living on his own property at Ipswich (Queensland). Anderson said that a few years ago he was working on a dairy near Beaudesert (Queensland). His eldest sister lived in the township. One night he dreamed he was standing by a deep pool of water and an airplane flying overhead suddenly nose-dived into the pool and disappeared without leaving a ripple. He dreamed then that the springs about Beaudesert began to flow unceasingly and he and a dream companion were soon in water up to their chests. He remarked to his companion, "I think our time's up."

He remembered the dream clearly on waking. He said the recollection of it was like the memory of a real experience. Due to the personal significance to him of dreaming of water, the dream caused him some concern and he said to a friend, "I think there's something wrong with my sister. She's pretty sick."

During that morning a police officer from Beaudesert drove out to the dairy and told Anderson that his sister had died at six o'clock that morning. She had been well the last time he had heard of her.

On a more recent occasion (August, 1953) when Anderson was working at Glenell Grove, some miles from Ispwich, he had a vivid dream of a great, raging flood, muddy and with a number of logs floating in it. He interpreted this dream as meaning that something was amiss with his family at Ipswich. During the morning a telegram arrived saying that his father was seriously ill in Ipswich Hospital.

Anderson then went to Ipswich and visited his father, taking it in turns with his brother to watch at his father's bedside. One night shortly afterward he again dreamed that he was standing by a pool. He dived in. The water seemed endlessly deep and he failed to reach the bottom. When he returned to the surface he saw his father standing on the bank of the pool. On waking he interpreted the dream as a death sign. His father did, in fact, die during the day.

Such experiences as those quoted may be viewed from the aboriginal point of view in this way: as their acculturation proceeds and they adopt Western ways of life and outlook, their psychic experiences diminish little and are not much reduced in intensity, but change in nature, losing tribal and magical significance and taking on those characteristics which are typical of the white pattern.

Immediately the question must come to mind as to whether, with their assimilation into the white community, the aborigines' sophistication will lead to an inhibition of psychic awareness. Magic has impressed my wife and me as being that aspect of aboriginal culture which will survive when others die out. We think that, while the aborigines retain racial identity, their psychical experiences will be more frequent, more profound, and in general more reliable than ours.

A New York nurse, plagued and gifted with psychic abilities, was a source of irritation and wonder to relatives and friends. The author has written widely on psychic phenomena. Her latest book is Prominent American Ghosts.

THE RELUCTANT PSYCHIC

Susy Smith

Student Nurse Helen Phillips leaped out of bed at three o'clock in the morning. She had just dreamed that one of her patients was standing beside his bed in Dellview Hospital in a curiously transparent condition, looking down with an amazed expression at his own body.

Helen knew from previous experience that her dreams usually carried definite significance. She phoned the hospital and told the nurse in charge of Ward K: "Mr. Rogers . . . Bed 15 . . . hurry, he just died."

The night nurse was more annoyed than startled. She had visited the ward shortly before. It had been as calm as a roomful of sick people can ever be. And she didn't appreciate an anonymous caller telling her how to run her business in the middle of the night.

But she walked down the corridor anyway, just to make sure. She came to Ward K . . . to Bed 15. The patient was dead.

Miss Phillips never told anyone that it was she who had phoned. In the days that followed, she listened quietly as excited hospital talk swirled around the mysterious night call reporting a patient's sudden death.

But how, in her sleep at home, had she been aware of what had happened at the hospital? She says that all her life she has received authentic information in inexplicable ways. And if she had her way, nobody would ever know about it.

Even though she has a gift shared by relatively few, Helen has never considered it a blessing. To her it has been a curse, for it sets her apart. Those who know of her apparently psychic talent look upon her as a curiosity. She dislikes the twitting, the skepticism, and the open-mouthed wonder which her gift so frequently arouses; yet frequently she feels obliged to reveal it. When the building porter complains of having lost his key, and Helen can plainly see a mental image of it, lodged under a certain chip in a wood pile, naturally she must tell him. And when subsequently the porter points her out as "the lady who found my key by seeing a picture of it inside her head," she feels thoroughly uncomfortable.

Once a young friend sadly reported the loss of her sorority pin, and Helen couldn't help telling her that it was hidden under a leaf in a yard ten blocks away. She herself went there, picked up the leaf . . . and there was the pin. But since then she's always wondered if her friend might not have thought she'd put the pin there in the first place, just as a trick.

At other times, of course, Helen Phillips can be well satisfied with her exploits.

"Once when I lived in a nurses' home, I left my watch in the lavatory," she relates. "And when I remembered and went back for it an hour later, it was gone. There were dozens of girls who lived there, but I knew instinctively that none of them had taken it. I went straight to a room which was only used by the woman porter." Going to a dusty cupboard, Helen knelt down, reached to the back, and pulled out a shoe. "In the toe of it was my watch," she explains.

If it is difficult to understand why she feels anything so fortuitous could produce problems. Miss Phillips explains that it's because nobody but her mother has ever been in sympathy with her. But in her highly respected Virginia family tree there had been an aunt who was known throughout the countryside as a clairvoyant. Helen's mother early recognized similar characteristics in her youngest offspring. She observed in Helen, even before her second year, a tendency to poke the air with her fingers as she tried to caress the "pretty things" she saw about her.

At five, Helen became aware that others could not see many of the beauties she saw. So she learned not to talk about them for fear of being ridiculed. She recalls psychically "knowing" where her mother's lost thimble was hiding, but being afraid to say for fear her mother might think she'd stolen it. As she grew older and became more aware of the oddness of her powers, she deliberately tried to conceal them. Yet her sisters always considered her "peculiar," and the three cousins with whom she chummed in her teens used to say of their pet secrets, "No use telling Helen! She knows it anyway . . ."

Helen says she wasn't particularly bright in school. But she managed to know most of the answers by being able to picture the textbook right in front of her.

This worked happily for her when she read "Hiawatha" for the first time at 3 P.M. one afternoon and recited the whole poem that night on stage before a gathering of nine hundred. She wasn't frightened, because "I knew if I followed instructions I'd have help." And her instructions, received mentally from whom or what she did not know, were to take her glasses off, to keep her eyes fixed on the wall at the back of the auditorium, and not to get stage fright. As she puts it, "They showed me the pages of the book in a golden light and I just read the words."

This odd habit caused her trouble later when she was taking an extracurricular psychology course at Columbia University. On one occasion, the professor drew a diagram on the blackboard, gave the class five minutes to observe it, and then erased it. One week later, when the students went to the board to produce it from memory, the teacher refused to accept Helen's too-accurate drawing, assuming she must have made a copy to hide away and study. Actually, Helen now says, she could see the diagram on the blackboard as it had been originally, and she was merely tracing the lines with chalk.

Some years later when Miss Phillips taught nursing at Fordham University, she did not use notes, but recalled assignments—page and line of the text—by seeing the book mentally.

Asked how this works—when it works—she doesn't know. She is practically sure that it can't be called photographic memory, and it certainly isn't total recall. What she "gets" psychically is most frequently in the form of pictures, sometimes brilliantly colored and sometimes gray. Occasionaly she feels as if someone were telling her the information. And sometimes she just seems to know a fact without having been at all aware of receiving it.

"Very often," Miss Phillips says, "I get an audible warning, sounding like a crack of static electricity, and then I know to look for a big square of light on which the picture is shown. But sometimes just yellow, red, or green lights appear."

All these sights and sounds seem to occur without her desire or her conscious coöperation, but she admits they've helped her out of many an awkward situation. They have gotten her into a few, too.

This sometimes happens when she predicts unpleasant events. The urge to read the cards may come over her suddenly, as if some invisible person were standing beside her insisting that she pass on certain information, and when she gives a reading with this kind of encouragement she's very good at it. Even though what she says may not always be popular.

One evening in the spring of 1957 she tucked her patient in for the night, walked out of the room where she was nursing on special duty, and saw a deck of cards on a desk in the hall. She picked them up on impulse and said to Nurse Randolph, who was sitting there, "Come on, I'll tell your fortune." They went into the lounge. Helen spread out the cards and said: "You are going to be involved with a toe. A friend of yours will be grief-stricken for a dear one very soon. And you're going to lose a small piece of metal from your watch which will cost four dollars to replace."

Mrs. Randolph wasn't particularly impressed with this reading, as who would be? What kind of fortune was that, without one single blonde king or dark jack or jealous queen? But about fifteen minutes later, when she asked an orderly to get something for her, he pulled a heavy drawer out too far and dropped it on his foot, mangling his big toe. The nurse rushed him to the accident ward and indeed was considerably "involved with a toe" for some time. Then, the next day, a friend's fiance was critically injured in a wreck, and Mrs. Randolph lost the stem of her watch. When the bill came to four dollars, she said, "That Phillips, I could kill her."

It's not surprising that this psychic is reluctant to read cards, if instead of getting her palm crossed with silver for her brilliant foresight, she is blamed for the things that happen.

Her curiosity aroused by the Randolph reading, a practical nurse named Jones came to Helen with the deck of cards, and the first thing Helen told her was: "You are going to have news from out of town that a friend has just had a baby with a club foot, and it will cost forty-five dollars to buy shoes for it." Miss Jones met a friend a few days later who told her this exact—and unusual—information.

Miss Phillips' powers don't depend upon a deck of cards, however. There's the time she met a nurse in the hall and said to her, "Get back to your room! Your patient is falling out of bed." The nurse hurried back, to find the man already on the floor. Helen hopes that her compulsion to make this sort of remark isn't talked about too freely. "For," she grumbles, "if the doctors knew I did anything like that, they'd laugh me right out of the hospital."

Here is a person whose entire philosophy is materialistic, based on her knowledge of medical science. Yet she illustrates, in her own experience, many concepts which most of the medical profession find difficult to accept. It is no wonder she wishes to remain anonymous, because her professional reputation is of great value to her. She has held responsible positions for many years, having been medical or obstetrical supervisor in several New York hospitals, nursing arts instructor, and charge nurse of floors countless times.

Now, at sixty-two, she is doing special duty nursing, devoting her spare time at home to sewing, or reading an occasional escapist-type paperback book. She has never read anything on psychic research which might explain the unusual qualities she exhibits, and she has no interest in the reasons for or the exploration of her own psychic talents.

Miss Phillips has studied enough psychology to recognize that there are those who would claim her phenomena to be entirely subjective, coming from within her own subconscious mind. She doesn't accept that theory, however, for she firmly believes her psychic powers are connected in some way with spirit survival. She has never thought of herself as a medium, would not dream of consenting to sit for development of mediumship, and is always shy of mentioning her conviction of the presence of spirit entities. Yet she says she has been forced to her conclusion because of the deceased personalities who have shown themselves to her, and the information they've given her.

One night she was sure that she saw a friend who had died seven years before, who told her to go to the doctor for an immediate examination because she had a growth she didn't suspect. She followed instructions and had an operation which saved her life.

Then there is the experience already related . . . her knowledge that patient 15, Ward K, had just died in the hospital. But it is her story of "Uncle Henry" that most nearly stands scrutiny as an event of an evidential nature.

Helen's sister Mabel is a witness to the fact that once, when they were vacationing in Florida, Helen announced: "Uncle Henry's dead." Mabel replied, "Oh, Helen, stop your foolishness. If I had your imagination I'd write a book."

But Helen was by this time fascinated by a picture that seemed to her to be projected on the side wall of the room, showing her Uncle Henry reenacting the scene of his accidental death. Walking across a field, he saw a big dark stranger carrying off one of his young sheep. He attacked the man, they struggled on an overhang of the river, and suddenly the piece of earth they were on dropped off into the water. The thief swam across the river with the sheep, but Uncle Henry was drowned.

As she saw this picture, Helen became convinced that her uncle was showing her how his death had occurred so that she could tell his wife he hadn't killed himself deliberately and left her alone with numerous debts. Her sister Mabel thought it was all nonsense, until the home-town paper arrived a few days later . . . with the report that their Uncle Henry had taken his life by jumping into the river.

Helen was pleased when her uncle's wife and children accepted her version of the accident. She was also glad when inquiry revealed that a band of gypsies had been camped across the river on the day he died. Any kind of corroboration of her psychic capabilities, while not in the least necessary to her belief in them, makes them more acceptable to other people.

In fact, in discussing this with her, it seems obvious that Miss Phillips is beginning to feel her occasional opportunity to soften the blow of death for a friend is almost recompense enough for the trouble her psychic sense causes her. She has concluded that this talent has its values after all . . . and that if enough scientific investigation is brought to bear on the subject, the world may some day know that death is not final.

Savage Indians became dangerous hazards on the Texas frontier; a scalped settler's life was saved only by a recurring accurate and simultaneous vision of his plight on the part of a neighbor who consciously believed him dead.

OR WAS IT A DREAM?

F. E. Wade

One of the first settlers in the now thickly populated area surrounding Austin, the capital of Texas, was Reuben Hornsby and wife Sarah, with several small children.

Mr. Hornsby was a man of means and built a substantial residence protected by a stockade from hostile Indians. This residence was the outpost of civilization for the then scantily settled Texas. The nearest neighbor, Josiah Wilbarger, was located seven miles down the twisting Colorado River.

Mr. Hornsby was an astute businessman; Mrs. Hornsby a wonderful hostess and hospitality radiated from their home. It became a stopping place for homeseekers to the vicinity. Mr. Hornsby and Mr. Wilbarger were both surveyors, and became sort of good-willers for the section, welcoming and helping locate newcomers.

In August of 1833, Mr. Wilbarger rode over to his neighbor and friend Hornsby's house to escort a party of four men in a land locating trip. The men's names were Strother, Christian, Standifer, and Haynie.

About noon, some four miles northwest of present day Austin, they spied an Indian, on horseback, on a distant hill watching them. Mr. Wilbarger made friendly signs and started riding toward him but the Indian galloped away.

The party traveled another mile until they came to a spring and against Mr. Wilbarger's better judgment, alighted, turned their horses loose to graze and sat down to rest and eat their lunch.

Without warning they were attacked by a group of some fifty Indians, expert with bows and arrows. Strother was killed at once, Christian apparently mortally wounded, Wilbarger was arrowed in the hip and had fallen. The Indians moved in closer and the other two men, thinking their three companions killed, jumped on their horses and headed toward the Hornsby residence.

Although Wilbarger was badly wounded, he managed to rise, get behind a tree, using the other men's guns to defend himself but an arrow in the neck paralyzed him and he fell again. The shrieking, jubilant Indians gathered in to strip and scalp their victims. Wilbarger, apparently dead, was perfectly helpless but was conscious of all that transpired. His clothes were pulled off and a knife passed entirely around his head and the scalp torn off. He afterwards said while he suffered no pain it sounded like a loud clap and roar of thunder.

He lay in a dreamy state of semiconsciousness the rest of the day and all night. At intervals he tried to crawl for help. Visions flitted through his mind bordering on the marvelous and supernatural.

He later affirmed that during the night, while resting against a tree, his sister, Margaret (Mrs. Margaret Clifton of Florissant, St. Louis County, Missouri) whom he was to learn months later had died the day before in Missouri, appeared to him saying:

"Brother Josiah, you are too weak to go on by yourself. Remain here and before the sun sets friends will come to take you in." And she disappeared in the direction of the Hornsby residence despite his plea for her to stay with him.

The two escaped men found their way back to Hornsby's and spread the alarm, stating their three companions were definitely killed.

About midnight, and it was later verified at about the same time of Mr. Wilbarger's visit by his sister, Mrs.

Hornsby jumped up in bed and awakened her husband, speaking so loud that the men in the next room heard her.

"Wilbarger is not dead," she said excitedly, "He sits against a large tree and is scalped. I saw him and know it is so!"

They all reassured her and remonstrated, even ridiculed her dream and all again returned to bed.

About three o'clock, she again sprang up under intense excitement, repeating the former statement and added:

"I saw him again. As sure as God lives, Josiah Wilbarger is alive, scalped, and sits under a large tree by himself. I saw him as plainly as I now see you who are present. If you are not cowards, go at once or he will die."

"But," said one of the escaped men, "Mrs. Hornsby, I saw fifty Indians around his body and it is impossible for him to be alive."

"I don't care what you saw," replied the seemingly inspired Mrs. Hornsby, "I saw him as plainly as you could have, and I know he is alive. Go to him at once."

Her husband was hesitant, saying they were too few in number and she and the children would be in danger if left alone.

"Never mind us. We can take to the dogwood thicket and save ourselves. Go, I beg you, to poor Wilbarger."

The men argued they would have to wait for daylight and reinforcements, but she refused to return to bed and busied herself getting food ready so there would be no delay when daylight and help came. She begged them to hurry and pulled a sheet from her bed and said:

"Take this, you will have to bring him back on a litter, he cannot ride a horse."

After a search, the party found the other two bodies and with reverent ceremony buried them under a large tree. As Wilbarger had stumbled and crawled nearly a mile away, they spent some time locating him. He was naked and so covered with blood they hesitated to approach thinking he might be an Indian until he made himself known.

They wrapped him in the sheet the kind Mrs. Hornsby

had provided and placed him on a horse with Mr. Hornsby at back to hold him on.

Mrs. Hornsby was a good nurse and took care of Wilbarger until he was able to be moved on a stretcher to his own cabin. The two families forever remained the closest of friends, and both Mrs. Hornsby and Mr. Wilbarger repeatedly told the stories of their experiences that tragic night. They were of such high caliber and integrity, no one questioned the veracity of either, and the stories have come down through a century and a quarter as part of Texas' proud pioneer history.

Mr. Wilbarger's head never healed, though he lived eleven useful years afterward, reared a large family and became a prosperous citizen. His death came about accidentally, by striking his unhealed head against some timber while working in his cotton gin.

In 1936 the Texas Centennial Commission erected a marker at the homesite of the worthy Hornsby family.

Did you ever wish you had the gift of knowing tomorrow's events? This woman knew of dangers and death, sometimes as *they occurred—when she had no possible access to the information except through telepathy—and sometimes* before *they occurred.*

SURPRISES FROM ESP (formerly I KNEW THE FUTURE!)

Marie S. Bordner

I have had premonitions of accidents, which enabled me to save others from injury. I have had a "visit" from a dead person, who gave me a warning of something that was to happen to a mutual friend. I have been able to "read" facts and predictions about persons that I had never seen before.

However, I am not a medium, nor crystal gazer. I am an advertising copywriter, leading a normal, if hectic, business life. I did not seek these experiences—they sought me. Others may accept or reject the validity of the following stories. However, I *must* accept them. They happened to me! It took a definite experience, when I was in my teens, to prove to me without doubt that at times I had a power that went beyond the capacities of my normal, conscious mind.

One of my best friends was going to entertain her sister's school chums from a southern college—three girls whom we had never met. She asked me for some suggestions. She wanted to give a party with "a different angle." I told her I would give it some thought.

Going over some old magazines in the attic, I found an article on tea leaf reading which was coming into vogue in tea rooms throughout the country. This would be it,

I decided! I would pretend to read tea leaves for her guests.

I knew nothing about the subject and had heard of it but vaguely. I studied the simple directions and diagrams: a heart, formed by leaves, meant a romance. Crossed sticks were quarrels or a parting of the ways, etc. I could add lots of things young girls were interested in and were eager to believe, I thought, such as, "A dark man wants to meet you," or "A blond Adonis is secretly in love with you." This would be fun. I went gaily off to the party. They all gathered around the table, each one wanting to be first. I instructed them officiously (according to the magazine) "Turn the cup around three times for magic and turn it upside down." This was to loosen the massed leaves so that only the "fortune" would cling to the bottom and sides.

I took the first cup gingerly, hoping my glibness would not desert me. I stared into it earnestly while I tried to think of something which could apply personally to the bright-eyed girl opposite me. Everybody waited expectantly. "What a fraud you are," I thought to myself.

And then suddenly I had a lot of things to say. The first had to do with the past, which was risky because it had to be true, but somehow I knew it was. "You started to go on a short trip today, but when you were half way there you changed your mind and went elsewhere."

She answered "Yes."

Sentence after sentence followed while the girls sat there spellbound. "One of you will get a telegram to return home sooner than expected," I said. (The next day, the telegram arrived.)

My hostess began giving me frantic signals to join her in the kitchen, but I couldn't get away. Finally, she said, "Just a minute, girls, I want Marie to help me with something."

When the swinging door closed behind us she grasped my arm. "'Where are you getting this stuff?" she demanded. "Did Edith (her sister) call you up?"

I shook my head, "No, it just occurs to me and I say it!"

"Well that is utterly amazing! It's all true!"

I must have turned white, for she took a decanter from

a cupboard and poured me some brandy while I tried to still the trembling of my limbs. My Roman Catholic upbringing led me to disapprove of fortune tellers, soothsayers, etc. My own cup of tea and a piece of delicious cake were left untouched on the table. I asked to be excused to a chorus of protests. My friend, who was considerably worried by my reaction, wanted to drive me the four blocks to my home but I refused. I had to be alone to think this over, to try to assimilate what the night had revealed.

Years later, when I learned more about extrasensory perception, I was no longer so full of fear and guilt feelings. Then I recalled another experience from my early life that was also, no doubt, an example of ESP.

I met a young man and we became good friends. We both had inquiring minds and we loved to have long discussions about serious matters. We spent many hours together, when he could get away from the many chores on his father's farm and his job as a rural mail carrier.

One night I was saying my prayers on my knees at the side of my bed, as was my custom, when suddenly seemingly without volition, I leaped to my feet and cried out, "Oh, David, don't!"

A moment later I found myself standing against the opposite wall, trembling violently. Much puzzled and upset, I wondered if I could be losing my mind. I crawled into bed but could not relax. I noticed the clock on the table; it read 11:15.

The next night I could scarcely wait for David to arrive. The episode of the night before had been too vivid, too disturbing, not to have some significance. Certainly it was connected with him.

When he stepped inside the door the first thing I said was, "What were you doing last night at eleven o'clock?"

A strange and wondering look passed over his face. "Petite"—his nickname for me—"you kept me from committing a murder last night!"

On his job Dave carried a gun for the protection of the mail. He was driving home late from an errand in another town when a car overtook his and a man called out for him to stop. Dave stopped, thinking someone needed help. The stranger jumped from his car; coming toward Dave he started to hurl insults and obscenities at him. Dave was accused of unbelievable things and suddenly he lost his temper completely. The man made a move toward his back pocket and Dave pulled his gun from the glove compartment of his car. He had his finger on the trigger ready to pull when—in his own words: "Petite, I swear at that moment your face came between us as plainly as I see you now!"

He was so startled that he dropped his arm. The headlights of a car coming up the road flicked over his face and the man stepped back in surprise. "Why you're not the fellow I thought you were!" he said. He leaped into his car and drove away, evidently afraid of what Dave would do about such an ill-advised incident. But Dave was lost in wonder at the apparition of me that he had just seen.

During World War II, four of my nephews were fighting at one time. Two in the Pacific area and two in the European theater. One of these boys—named Lee—was closer to me than the others, possibly because he had spent more time with my family and me.

One evening while resting after work, I suddenly saw, in my mind, a picture of Lee—running desperately as from some great danger. I could see plainly that he was headed for a doorway with an arched portal. It seemed terribly important to me that he reach it, but before he did so the picture faded and another took its place. Some men were putting Lee in the back of a vehicle which I could not see. I knew that in that blacked-out second Lee had been injured. Later this was confirmed by message and many months later by Lee himself. It happened just as I had seen it. He was running from a bomb—he was hit by a fragment and put in the back of a jeep.

Some years later, a different type of experience occurred to me. Living next door to me for many years was a friend named Alice, one of the sweetest persons I ever knew, and her aunt. Alice had been raised by this beloved aunt and uncle and trained for a career in music, which she loved. But ill fortune struck the family bringing many changes and she was forced to take an office job that she hated. Her life was one frustration after another. Finally she acquired cancer and died of it.

After her death I was sitting in the garden where we had spent so many evenings talking. We had discussed ideas, beliefs, faiths, philosophies—anything which might be a means through which she could become resigned to the death which she knew was near.

It was the most beautiful time of day—twilight. Peace seemed to have settled upon the earth. The perfume of lilies and petunias around me was strong. White night moths fluttered from flower to flower. Suddenly I was struck with an awareness; the world around me seemed to recede and I waited in intense anticipation for something. Then into my mind came one sentence: "Tell Aunt Hattie to be careful of the stairs."

It was urgently clear and precise. I whispered "Alice!" and waited, holding my breath, but nothing else came to me. The mimosa tree ruffled its branches in the wind, and a sleepy bird peeped.

I knew I had to deliver this message—it was urgent—so I went next door and told her aunt that I had dreamed it, afraid she would think me demented if I told her I was wide awake. To my surprise the old lady, who was more than eighty years old, took it as a matter of course. "Oh," she replied, "Alice was always afraid I would fall down those back stairs."

A few weeks later she got up in the night, mistook one door for another and fell down the entire flight of stairs. So critically injured was she they thought she might not recover. She had to remain in bed for weeks.

One day the grocery boy delivered my order and a warning for him suddenly flashed into my mind . . . but how to tell him? After some verbal give-and-take I asked him: "Do you go out Route 42 and pass the old Harker estate?"

"Not on my regular route," he replied. "Why?"

"There's a railroad bridge with an abrupt approach to it, isn't there?"

"Yes," he answered expectantly.

"Well," I finished lamely, "it's a dangerous place and

if I were you, I'd be careful when I go by there. You could easily have an accident."

"Yeh, I guess you could at that." By his expression he evidently thought I was a nut. Well, I told myself, you tried, anyway. What else could I do?

About a week later when he came with my order he said. "Mrs. Bordner, you must be psychic or something. You know that bridge you mentioned last week? I was going out there to visit a friend and as I came close to that bridge, I remembered what you said, and I slowed up. It's a good thing I did too, for a guy was coming up the other side at about sixty. He swerved as he came on and if I hadn't slowed up when I did he would have hit me head-on! Thanks for the warning."

He drove off laughing at what he thought was a mere coincidence. I looked after him, turning a can of beans over and over. What did I have in my hands?

An earlier episode calls attention to the fact that some of the things I said and wrote half-seriously could turn out to be prophetic. On this occasion I made three statements in jest that came true twenty years later.

I had gone for a drive with some girls I knew but slightly. We drove through a small mining town in the vicinity of my home town and discovered that a dance was going on. Having nothing better to do, we parked and went in. The other girls spotted some boys from another town that they knew and I didn't. They danced gaily off with them, leaving me stranded against the wall.

Presently I spied a tall young man coming in. Among the miners and small town boys he stood out strikingly. He wore an expensive-looking suit, an immaculate white shirt, and had a sophisticated bearing. He looked as if he had strayed out of the pages of *Esquire*. He spotted me and came down to ask me to dance. On my tip-toes I could just about see over his shoulder. Heads turned, eyebrows went up, lips formed the question, "Where did you find him?" I was the envy of the other girls.

He began to ask me questions. "You're not from this town, are you?" I shook my head.

"Where are you from?" he continued.

I wanted to appear "big town," as I knew he was, so I said, "Philadelphia."

I had never been to Philadelphia except to pass through, but I hated it as I did all big cities at that time. It was just a bit of pretension, normal in a girl of my age.

His next question was: "Are you married?"

Embarked upon a fictional career, I decided to continue it. So, I replied, "No, I'm a widow."

He guessed that I was kidding, but he went along with the gag. "What did your husband die of—did you throw him down the steps?" He said this with a grin, for I was a five-foot, ninety-pound model.

"No," I said slowly, "He died of heart failure!" For some reason this sounded funny to us, and we both burst out laughing. The young man was in that vicinity to help plan a home for a world-famous millionaire and I never saw him again.

However, twenty years later I was living in Philadelphia; I was a widow; and my husband had died of heart failure!

A talented young fashion artist was on the staff of the large store where I was assistant advertising manager. We became very good friends and rode around constantly in her small sports car.

She was an ardent horsewoman and not only kept her own riding horse but also often exercised the various horses at her country club.

One day I was troubled by a premonition of danger to her from a horse. I tried to forget it as I knew she would only laugh at me. Besides, she was an expert rider who was afraid of no horse she had ever seen. She had been riding since she was eight years old.

Finally I asked her, "Do you ride a bay-colored horse, perhaps with some white through the mane, and an extra long tail?"

"Why, no," she answered. "There is no horse of that sort at the country club. Why do you ask?"

"Oh," I said, lamely, "I have a premonition of danger to you from such a horse. Please be careful."

Jane was the earthy type who lived for today and didn't trouble herself about tomorrow. "Oh, you and your notions!" she scoffed. "You're slightly 'teched' but I like you anyway!" And, laughing at my serious face, she drove away.

A week or so later she drove her car to the country club and was immediately hailed by the men from the stables:

"Hi, Jane!" they called. "We have a horse we want you to ride."

One of them went inside and came out with . . . the horse of my description. Jane stood there stupified.

"What's wrong with him?" she asked.

"Nothing!" they answered. "We just wanted to see if you could ride him."

She knew they were baiting her. They were fully aware of her riding ability and all the trophies she had won. But pride would not permit her to refuse to ride him. She got on him very warily, as she was considerably upset by the accuracy of my word picture.

The horse started off docilely enough, but she was on her guard. Suddenly he bolted. It took all her knowledge of horses to bring him under control. If she had not been forewarned she most surely would have been thrown.

She took him back to the stable and demanded to know what was wrong with him. The men, rather embarrassed, when they saw how shaken she was, told her this horse had been in a spill and pile-up of horses in a race and he had emerged so nervous that he was sent to the country club to recuperate.

She hurried to my home to tell me about it, very excited. When she was leaving, she turned at my gate and said, "Marie, you have some quality . . . I don't know what it is!" and, shaking her head she went down the walk. I gazed after her. I shook my head also. I did not know what it was either.

The horror passage of a book read by a friend, a doctor, miles away, appeared in a dream that same evening, with startling exactitude, to a man in Peekskill, New York.

"NAIL IT UP TIGHT!"

C. W. Weiant

While reports of telepathic dreams are no novelty and have been abundantly reported in psychoanalytic literature, the case which I am about to describe is of interest because it demonstrates unmistakably the capacity of the unconscious to pick up telepathic impressions while the recipient is fully conscious, the transmitted material not rising to the conscious level until after a considerable lapse of time (in this instance about seven hours) as the result of a dream.

On the night of Thursday, October 31, 1957, Dr. Jean Worth, a colleague of mine on the facility of the Chiropractic Institute of New York, who shares my interest in the paranormal, sat quietly in her New York apartment between the hour of 11 P.M. and midnight, browsing in a book entitled *Thirty Years among the Dead.* This book, written by a physician, Dr. Carl A. Wickland, a member of the Illinois State Medical Society, was published, without date, by the Spiritualist Press, Ltd., of 49 Old Bailey, London, E.C. 4. The doctor's wife was a medium. The section pertinent to this story reads as follows:

"Upon another occasion, when I had been appointed assistant demonstrator for a class in dissecting, the body of a colored man had been selected as a subject but the body had not been disturbed when, one evening, Mrs. Wickland became entranced, and a strange spirit speaking through her, exclaimed:

" 'You ain't goin' to cut on dis colored man, Boss!'

"I told him that the world called him dead; that he was not in his old body, but was now controlling a woman's body. He would not believe this, and when I showed him my wife's hands, saying they were not colored but white, he replied:

" 'I'se got whitewash on dem; whitewashin' is my business.'

"This spirit proved to be very obstinate, offering a variety of excuses and explanations rather than accept the truth, but he was finally convinced and departed."

While reading this passage, Dr. Worth was also thinking intently of me and wondering what my reaction to the story would be. At about seven o'clock of the following morning, October 31, I awoke from a very disagreeable dream. This is what I dreamed: the Chiropractic Institute of New York was offering a course in dissection. The demonstrator had just finished dissecting the body of a colored man. He then replaced the viscera and other parts of the cadaver which had been removed. The body was then laid in a wooden box. As the box was about to be nailed shut, the body suddenly began to stir and succeeded in rising. Horrified, I exclaimed, "Why, he's not dead!" Dr. Worth, who was standing beside me, countered with, "Don't be silly; it's just a bundle of reflexes." Then, with some difficulty, a group of students succeeded in subduing the seemingly animated cadaver and proceeded to nail up the box. One of the onlookers yelled, "Nail it up tight."

At this point I awoke, astonished that I should have had such an absurd dream.

Later in the day I was talking to Dr. Worth on the telephone and related the dream. "I can explain that dream," she said, and a few days later she brought me the Wickland book and indicated the passage I have quoted. The elements of correspondence between those lines and my dream are so striking that a causal relationship seems inescapable.

It should be added that at the time Dr. Worth was reading and thinking of me, I myself was sitting in my den at my home in Peekskill, working on the manuscript of a book in no way related to the occult.

What power forced Mrs. Paul out into a driving Minnesota snow storm to renew her husband's accident policy on the same day that he had *an accident, unknown to her, in the state of Washington?*

DOUBLE INDEMNITY

Val E. Paul

It was December 4, 1950, just past noon, and as I felt a little drowsy after eating, I decided to take a short nap at our home in Minnesota.

In a short while I was awakened suddenly by my own sobbing. Tears were streaming down my cheeks. I had just had the most frightening and realistic dream.

I saw my husband's limp figure being lifted and carried by two strangers. His face and jacket were smeared with dirt. I sat up on the edge of the couch and shook my head vigorously, but it was a trance from which I could not awaken. I wondered if I had slept long, and glancing at the clock, I noticed that it was just past one in the afternoon, Central Standard Time.

I began to wonder about my husband. He must have reached Seattle now, since he had left home two days before to look for work in Seattle or Tacoma. If he found work and a place to live, the children and I were to follow him later. I had not heard from him by mail as it takes five days to receive a letter from Seattle. I was determined not to worry.

As I rose and attempted to follow my usual household routine, the feeling of apprehension grew and dominated all my thinking. If he had been in an accident, I had better look for his insurance policy which I knew was about to expire. My family had been going through financial difficulties and if there had been an accident, we would need the insurance. I found the policy and sure enough, it was in its last day of grace. I would need twenty-five dollars to renew it, and that was all that I had for groceries and for the care of our two small children. I knew that I could not use this money.

I decided to try borrowing enough from my husband's father. He lived fifteen miles from my home, but at that moment a severe winter storm with drifts of snow made the road hazardous. It was already two-thirty and I doubted if I could make it over there and back to the insurance office in time to renew the policy.

Again I tried to reason that it was foolish to feel so certain about something with only a dream for backing. But a stronger force seemed to overpower my reason. I had to go, even though I feared the danger of driving through a storm with the children.

On the way to my in-laws, I decided that I had better not mention my dream. I would simply tell them that my husband had forgotten to leave enough money to cover his quarterly insurance payment. They lent me the money without any question, and I left immediately for the insurance office. I arrived there just before closing time. Relieved from worry, I drove home through the storm.

A week filled with anxiety passed, without any word from my husband. Finally, on December 9, a letter arrived in his handwriting. "At last he is well enough to write," I thought, and tore the envelope open with trembling hands. I read the following letter:

Tacoma, Washington
December 4, 1950

My dearest Val,

You will be very much surprised to learn that I've been in a bus accident. It happened between Seattle and Tacoma. I had decided to go and call on your Uncle Dan in Tacoma, to see if he could help me find a job. I didn't want him to think that I wanted to move in with him so I left my suitcase in the depot in Seattle. Then it turned out that he invited me to stay there until I found a job, and so I was returning to Seattle to pick up my suitcase when the accident occured.

A car driven by a woman ran head-on into the bus. The driver slammed on his brakes and the bus careened and landed on its side, scrambling all the passengers. The woman driver of the car was killed outright. This was a four-lane highway, and we were the only two vehicles on the road. It seemed incredible that an accident should happen under those circumstances.

I found myself lying in the aisle on my stomach with a big, burly passenger on top of my shoulders. He was lying crossways in the bus and had a badly broken leg, so he was unable to move until help came. It seemed ages before they took him off me, and when they did, my arms seemed to be paralyzed, and I too had to be lifted and carried out of the bus. I sure was dirty, my face was covered with smudges and my jacket was a mess.

My shoulder is badly bruised and I have a very stiff neck. Tomorrow I have to go to the hospital for a check-up to find out if I have any fractures. I'm plenty stiff and sore. Bus insurance will come in here, and by the way, look up my Travelers Insurance and see if it is still in force. Send me the number . . . I hope to see you by Christmas.

Love to you and the kids,
DADDY

He arrived home the day before Christmas, and we began to check the time of my dream and the accident. I wrote to the editor of *The Tacoma News Tribune* and he replied that the accident occurred on the Seattle-Tacoma highway shortly after 3 P.M. Pacific Coast Time, on Monday, December 4, 1950. My dream took place a little after 1 P.M. Central Standard Time. Thus my dream and the accident had occurred simultaneously.

As my husband had been riding on a public conveyance when the accident occurred, we were paid double indemnity by the insurance company. So it seemed that my telepathic warning had pierced the barrier of two thousand miles, to help us provide for our family in a time of danger and distress. I am now convinced that no distance is too great when the mind reaches out to protect those we love.

His day's work finished, and facing home-bound traffic, what caused Tommy Whittaker to return to Washington Street, in Boston? He must have sensed that his friend was in trouble, through telepathy, because they'd had no other contact. The authors are a prominent husband-and-wife team in psychological and parapsychological research.

BURIED ALIVE—SAVED BY TELEPATHY

Betty and Fraser Nicol

Like many people, Jack Sullivan had never given much thought to telepathy—he was much too busy supporting a family of five children and trying to build up his welding business in Stoneham, Massachusetts. It was not until June 14, 1955, when he came suddenly and painfully close to death, that the idea of some psychic connection between friends seemed more than a remote possibility to him.

As he told us in an interview three months after his brush with death, the fact that he is still alive to describe it may be the result of telepathy or of prayer, or both. But after an experience such as his, he does not believe—and perhaps others may not believe—that "mere coincidence" is a very plausible explanation.

In the late afternoon of June 14, Sullivan was alone in a 14-foot trench welding new 36-inch water pipes alongside busy Washington Street in the southwest section of Boston. By 4:30 P.M., the last pipe for the day had been laid in place by the power-shovel crew, who then stopped work, leaving Sullivan to finish welding the seam between the last two pipes in the trench.

The day was very hot. Sullivan finished his work on the inside joint, crawled out of the pipe, and started making the outside seam. He had about an hour's more work to do, he figured, and should finish by about six o'clock.

When he stopped a minute to adjust his welding rod, he noticed some children playing around his truck, parked nearby. The generator on the truck was running to furnish power for the welding. Thinking the children might hurt themselves, he chased them away.

He pulled the welding shield back down over his face and was about to resume welding when the calamity happened. There was no noise—no rumble—no warning—as tons of earth, clay and stones fell upon him from behind. The trench had caved in.

He was knocked down against the pipe in a more or less kneeling position. His legs were doubled up under him, his head was knocked against the pipe, his nose was smashed against the inside of the welding mask. At first he was conscious only of the searing pain in his right shoulder, which was jammed against the red hot weld he had been making on the pipes. He tried to edge away from the hot pipe, but the burden of earth on top of him held him tight against it. He managed to work his left hand up along his body to the shoulder and, wiggling his fingers, tried to get some of the dirt to fall down between the pipe and his burning shoulder. This maneuver was futile—he only burned his hand badly.

Though buried under the earth, he shouted for help, hoping the children might still be around and hear. But after a few shouts he became short of breath. He thought it best to take things easily and not use up the air around the mask too quickly. With the generator running on the truck, probably no one could have heard him anyhow, he realized.

He suddenly discovered his right hand was sticking straight up through the earth into the open air of the pit. He tried moving the hand around in hope that some air would come down to him. His fingers touched the welding rod lying on top of the dirt and he managed to get hold of it. Knocking it around above ground, he hoped to make noise enough to attract attention. But it was exhausting. And no one came.

Finding it increasingly difficult to get air, he tried to knock out the broken glass of the eye plate on the shield, but failed. A lucky thing he had the shield on, he thought (as he told us afterward). Without it, the dirt would have so covered his nose and mouth that he could not have breathed at all.

His entire hope now was to hold out long enough to be discovered; if darkness fell it did not seem likely that he would be found until too late. He wondered how long he'd been buried—it was hard to guess. He knew it must have been just about five o'clock when the trench fell in.

Busy Washington Street ran alongside the trench. Hundreds of homeward-bound motorists were only a few feet away, but the trench was so deep that a person in a passenger car would not be able to see down into it. Sullivan thought that his hand above the earth might be seen from the high cab of some passing truck. Or possibly a curious pedestrian would look in.

Afterwards he told of the things that ran through his mind while he was imprisoned there. He wondered how his family would fare if he didn't get out alive. He thought of each of his five children. "They seemed as clear as if they were standing right there" before him.

Then a vivid picture of Tommy Whittaker came into his mind. Whittaker was his best friend—a welder too, who had been working for Sullivan's welding company this spring. Whittaker, he knew, was working that day on another part of the water-main project some four or five miles away, near Route 128 in Westwood. Somehow Sullivan got the idea that Tommy Whittaker might help him.

Whittaker didn't even know that Sullivan was at the Washington Street job. Sullivan had planned to spend the day working in Chelsea, north of Boston. Nobody had worked on the Washington Street job for several weeks. The project there had been held up when the trench-cutting crews had run into rock ledges. Sullivan himself had not been informed of resumption of the pipe-laying there until noon that day. So he knew Whittaker would think he was still up north in Chelsea. But still, Sullivan had a very clear mental picture of his friend working near the golf course in Westwood a few miles away.

He tried to breathe slowly to save oxygen, and was thankful for the few air pockets around the big pipe which the dirt hadn't filled in solidly. The blood from his broken nose kept dropping into his throat, and it was harder and harder to breathe. There was nothing to do but lie there and pray and hope.

Farther south of Boston, in Westwood, Whittaker was welding more water pipes. Working with him was Danny, a welder from another company. They were welding overtime in order to finish up a seam before stopping for the night.

Welding becomes an automatic job (Whittaker later told us), so that all sorts of irrelevant things run through your mind and you hardly know you are working. Into Whittaker's mind, as he worked that afternoon, came the idea that he ought to go up to Washington Street and check. It was so vague he can hardly explain it. He felt that something was wrong. No particular person came to mind, only the persistent idea that he should go and check.

He got up and started to pack up his equipment.

"Where are you going?" asked Danny.

"I'm going up to the Washington Street job," answered Whittaker.

"There's nobody working up there now, is there?" said Danny.

"No, but I think I had better go."

"But we'll finish up here in half an hour," Danny pointed out.

"Well, I think I better go now. There might be something wrong." So he drove off, leaving Danny alone to finish up. It was about 5:30 P.M.

Usually when he quit work there, he went straight on to Route 128, the superhighway around Boston, and on home to Stoneham in the north. This night, he turned back into the heavy traffic and drove to Washington Street. He still doesn't know exactly why he did it—something seemed to be drawing him on.

At one point he saw a man he knew, another worker on the same large water-pipe project, and stopping to talk to him, Whittaker said he was on his way up to the other job on Washington Street. But the man said he didn't think anyone was working there. They talked for some ten minutes, then Whittaker said he'd better go on and check anyway.

Nearing the trenches on Washington Street (near DeSoto Road), he saw one of his company's trucks standing there with the generator running. He drew up behind it. No one was around. He got out and walked over to the trench. At first all he saw was dirt. Then he realized there had been a cave-in. Finally he saw the hand sticking out.

He leaped into the trench and started digging with his hands as fast as he could. He did not know who was buried, but thought it must be either Jack Sullivan or his brother. He tried to drag the earth away from the man's head. But his progress was painfully slow. He jumped up, ran across the street to a filling station, asked them to call the fire department, and ran back with a borrowed snow shovel to continue digging.

In only a few minutes the firemen came. It was twenty minutes more before they got him out. He was badly hurt, but still breathing. He was taken to the hospital, where he remained for several weeks.

Sullivan says, "When Tommy jumped into that hole, I felt the earth shake and knew help had come. Thank God."

It was 6:30 P.M. when he was lifted out. Whittaker had made the discovery about six, so his friend must have been buried over an hour. Sullivan's shoulder was very badly burned, and the doctors tell him he is not likely to have more than about 25 percent use of that shoulder and arm. His left hand was burned, his nose was broken, a bone in one foot and another near his knee were broken also. But he feels lucky to be alive. His gratitude to Whittaker is boundless.

Whittaker says he cannot explain what made him go back that day. He drove four or five miles out of his way, passing several intersections that would have taken him directly home. He had not seen the particular section of trench where the cave-in happened and did not know anyone was working there. The feeling was not even one of urgency. He simply felt he ought to go to that place. He didn't know why but he knew he wouldn't be comfortable until he did.